MW01641392

CLINICAL NOTES
ON
GROUP-ANALYTIC PSYCHOTHERAPY

D. WILFRED ABSE

M.D., B.Sc. (Wales), D.P.M. (London)
F.A.P.A., F.B.Ps.S., F.R.C.Psych.

Professor of Psychiatry, University of Virginia
Faculty Member: The Washington Psychoanalytic Institute and
The Washington School of Psychiatry

UNIVERSITY PRESS OF VIRGINIA
CHARLOTTESVILLE

THE UNIVERSITY PRESS OF VIRGINIA

First published 1974

ISBN: 0–8139–0508–7
Library of Congress Card Number: 73–81767

Printed in Great Britain

For Kate Abse

Acknowledgments

MY greatest single debt for help on this book is to Virginia Kennan, Editorial Assistant of the Department of Psychiatry, who, in addition to offering sound criticism at every stage of preparation, carried part of the burden of research of the relevant literature. I am also heavily indebted to analytic patients, both those in group and in individual analytic therapy, and to their families and physicians; and to many residents in training in psychiatry.

D. W. A.

Charlottesville, 1972

The author and publishers make grateful acknowledgment for permission to quote copyright material as listed below.

To the Hutchinson Publishing Group Ltd. for material from *Anatomy of judgment*, by M. L. Johnson Abercrombie.

To Grove Press, Inc. and Faber & Faber Ltd. for material from *Waiting for Godot*, by Samuel Beckett. Copyright © 1954 by Grove Press, Inc.

To the Macmillan Publishing Co., Inc. and Thames and Hudson Ltd. for material from *The informed heart*, by Bruno Bettelheim.

To the Macmillan Publishing Co., Inc. and Routledge & Kegan Paul Ltd. for material from *Suicide*, by Emile Durkheim.

To Sigmund Freud Copyrights, Ltd., The Institute of Psycho-analysis, The Hogarth Press Ltd., and Liveright Publishing Corporation for permission to quote from 'Group Psychology and the Analysis of the Ego' in Volume XVIII of *The standard edition of the complete psychological works of Sigmund Freud*, revised and edited by James Strachey.

To George Allen & Unwin Ltd. and International Universities Press Inc. for material reprinted from *Therapeutic group analysis*, by S. H. Foulkes.

To Yale University Press for material from *Seven plays of Maxim Gorky*, translated by Alexander Bakshy in collaboration with Paul S. Nathan.

Quotation from *The Greek way* by Edith Hamilton reprinted with the permission of the publishers, W. W. Norton & Co., Inc., New York. Copyright © 1930, 1943 by W. W. Norton & Co., Inc. Copyright renewed 1958 by Edith Hamilton.

From *The language of ideas* by William F. Irmscher and E. R. Hagemann, copyright © 1963 by the Bobbs–Merrill Co., Inc., reprinted by permission of the publisher.

To *Modern drama* for material from 'Truth and the Dramatic Mode in Modern Theater', by Alvin B. Kernan, © 1958 by *Modern drama.*

To Cornell University Press for material from *Modernism in modern drama*, by Joseph Wood Krutch, © 1953 by Cornell University.

To the Pirandello Estate and E. P. Dutton & Co., Inc., for permission to quote from the book *Naked masks: five plays*, by Luigi Pirandello. Edited by Eric Bentley. (Copyright © 1922, 1952 by E. P. Dutton & Co., Inc. Renewal 1950 by Stefano, Fausto and Lietta Pirandello. Published by E. P. Dutton & Co., Inc., in a paperback edition and used with their permission.)

To the University of Pennsylvania Press for material from *The drama of Luigi Pirandello*, by Domenico Vittorini, copyright © 1935 by the University of Pennsylvania Press.

To Cassell & Co. Ltd. and The Viking Press, Inc., for material from *Mental healers: Franz Anton Mesmer, Mary Baker Eddy, Sigmund Freud*, by Stefan Zweig, translated by Eden and Cedar Paul. (Copyright 1932, © 1960 by The Viking Press, Inc. Reprinted by permission of The Viking Press.)

Preface

INTEREST in what actually takes place in group psychotherapy is no longer limited to professionals engaged in psychiatric practice or psychological investigation. Highly diverse possibilities of self-discovery within many kinds of groups have been widely publicized. Many people now wistfully believe that group psychotherapy offers a solution for their most personal difficulties, whereas others turn to it simply for the improvement of the skills needed in corporate business management. Reports of excesses in encounter groups may pique either salacious curiosity or outrage; to many, group psychotherapy is but one aspect of ambient bold and iconoclastic social experimentation.

Some few psychiatrists have unfortunately taken the view—one uncritically adopted by many clinical psychologists—that individual psychosis may represent a useful and heroic reaction against a sick world. In this era of social experimentation, deviation in the individual may, indeed, be popularly designated as evidence of an enviably advanced state of awareness, while unacceptable regulative community attitudes are attributed to the ills of society. Admittedly, these confusions contain elements of truth—in turbid suspension. But medical practitioners should not be misled into advising widely deviant or basically unstable patients to participate in groups led by self-styled human relations experts, since all too often such patients decompensate further in "growth center" group activity. The leaders of these groups often in fact lack the knowledge necessary to screen such high-risk patients, and many harbor distorted notions of how to deal with them once they join in any of the action-oriented groups now epidemic. Experience in group-analytic groups helps greatly to clarify the desiderata of group therapy, and to warn of its limitations and perils.

This discussion of *group-analytic psychotherapy* will take into account the range of circumstances in which group interplay is used for the resolution of psychic problems, and trace the history of this modality. It will also outline for the professional the basic essentials for practicing the art of group-psychoanalytic psychotherapy, and offer criteria for referring a patient for this treatment. It reflects my observation of the professional needs of the several generations of residents in psychiatry I have taught in two university departments of psychiatry. Its brevity recognizes the limitations of time and energy with which the resident is inevitably faced.

Twenty-five years of experience has led me to believe that group-analytic psychotherapy can also be conducted well by paramedical practitioners of sound character who have a good background in clinical psychology or psychiatric social work. However, it seems important to me that each such non-medical therapist have a personal psychoanalysis as well as experience participating as a member in a group-analytic therapy group, and that he practice in close collaboration with physicians. Persons trained in group-analytic psychotherapy can contribute significantly to meeting the increasing demand for technically trained workers in the field of mental health. Moreover, such a contribution could have an impact on our entire culture and go far beyond benefits to the individuals treated, just as Lawrence S. Kubie (1971) has suggested in his discussion of what might be expected were a new profession of psychotherapy *per se* soundly established.

The field of *group encounter* includes at present many wild excursions; participants attracted to them by the hope of relief for their neurotic suffering postpone psychiatric consultation and evade or defer a referral for appropriate and adequate psychotherapy. Encounter groups have no doubt sprung up because of the widespread loneliness resulting from the grossly inadequate human communication within our technologically advanced yet fragmented society. The help they provide is often questionable. They may indeed disrupt warmly satisfying interpersonal association in family life as often as they promote it.

Family therapy is another recently developed type of group therapy, provided to reduce the already severe and steadily increasing strain the institution of the family is undergoing in our society. Any effort to shore up the family directly as a nurturing and integrative social institution is laudable. However, transference manifestations may be dealt with in group-analytic psychotherapy more adequately, and this advantage should be weighed against the wider therapeutic leverage provided the therapist specifically in family therapy by face-to-face relationships of all available family members in each session. With these and cognate considerations we will concern ourselves in the pages which follow.

Contents

Foreword

IT is with friendly affection that I respond to Wilfred Abse's request to write a few words as an introduction to this book. It is natural that one wishes to say something positive on such an occasion, but it is not so frequent that one can do so with such complete conviction as is here the case.

This book offers a condensed and lucid account of group-analytic psychotherapy with which this author is thoroughly familiar through his own intensive experience. He places group analysis fairly and adequately into its context and in relation to other forms of group psychotherapy which have been developed. What is more, while informing us so interestingly and lucidly about the present scene, Dr. Abse makes full use of the new perspective which group-analytic psychotherapy and its theory affords. This is as it should be, for this historical period with its specific psychopathological and psychotherapeutic problems is not one to look back upon—it has only just begun.

To envisage such a task one has to be immersed in this subject by daily intensive practice and thought, but not submerged in it to an extent that would not allow one to see its broader meaning in the light of the totality of human existence. The author integrates in a scientific spirit his rich insight into relevant technical literature and his sensitive appreciation of what literary writers tell us. Thus it is not surprising that his work can teach us so much and tells us its message in a style which makes it a pleasure to read.

I have known Wilfred Abse since the Northfield days in World War II and we resumed our acquaintance after the war. It was a severe loss to see him emigrate overseas. Our common interests and professional contacts had made us into personal friends. Thus our cooperation did not break down. Some of his personal observations in this book concerning myself are taken from a recent correspondence which continues. Perhaps geographical distance has made it easier for Wilfred Abse to express a more positive attitude to my work than is sometimes possible for those who are in more intimate personal contact. In this way I might be compensated for the loss of his continued presence.

At any rate this book and its warm and genuine appreciation of my own contribution, not so much explicit as implicit, gives me great personal pleasure. I am sure it will have the success it so richly deserves and I can promise the reader that he will be rewarded for his attention, each according to his own qualifications.

S. H. F.

London, August 1972

WHEN Croesus the rich, the King of Lydia, sent to Delphi to find out if he would succeed in a war against Persia and paved his way by magnificent gifts, any priests in the world except the Greeks would have made their profit for their church by an intimation that the costlier the offering the surer his success, but the only answer the Greek holy of holies gave him was that by going to war he would destroy a great empire. It happened to be his own, but, as the priestess pointed out, she was not responsible for his lack of wit, and certainly there was no intimation that if he had given more, things would have turned out better. The sentences which Plato says were inscribed in the shrine at Delphi are singularly unlike those to be found in holy places outside of Greece. *Know thyself* was the first, and *Nothing in excess* the second, both marked by a total absence of the idiom of priestly formulas all the world over.

From *The Greek Way* by Edith Hamilton

PART I

BASIC PRINCIPLES, PRACTICAL CONSIDERATIONS AND APPLICATIONS

I Preliminary Definition and Brief Historical Perspective

THIS country is in an anxiety-ridden era, with a rising tide of emotional and mental disorder. Anxiety neuroses, obsessional and phobic states, hysterical and psychosomatic disorders, as well as borderline and major psychoses, are common. There is also much depressive misery associated with those chronic deformations of character in which little overt anxiety appears except in crisis. This tide of neurotic and psychotic disorder is rising in a period of "community psychiatry" during which community cooperation in the amelioration of such suffering is being energetically sought by mental health professionals—and in a period that follows and incorporates one in which effective treatment by psychotropic drugs and electroconvulsive therapy was developed, the "therapeutic milieu" promoted, and psychotherapy improved. The groundwork for these effective treatments had in turn been laid by the humanistic endeavors pioneered by Pinel and others toward the end of the last century, and the scientific studies of neurosis and psychosis pursued by Kraepelin and Freud and their followers in the beginning of this.

Group therapy has now come to assume major importance in the delivery of psychiatric care. The therapeutic group is composed of people who have in common the quest for the relief of suffering; it meets with a psychotherapist at regular intervals. There are many forms of group therapy, just as there are of individual psychotherapy. Giles W. Thomas (1943) tried to categorize group therapies by opposing the polarities of the "analytic" approach to group therapy on the one hand and the "repressive-inspirational" approach on the other. Some repressive-inspirational approaches, however, not only stimulate the partial release of previously unconscious urges and emotions, but catalyze some degree of insight into the meaning of these new experiences. Just as in individual psychotherapy, the dichotomy of "covering" and "uncovering" types is not sharp. Every psychoneurosis has mental conflict as its basis. A change in the dynamic relations of the constituents of conflict can dissipate the symptoms of the neurosis. In principle, as Otto Fenichel (1945) pointed out, amelioration of immediate neurotic suffering can be accomplished in two ways: by either an increase in or an annulment of the defense—that is, by further covering or uncovering of the elements in conflict. However, an undoing of a repression may be used for the intensification of another repression, so that a psychotherapy may be, unwittingly or wittingly, covering and uncovering in varying proportions. In individual analytic psychotherapy the sustained uncovering technique, combined with a working-through of the opened conflicts with the psychotherapist, results in the gradual resolution of conflict. The process necessitates basic personality change. It is accomplished against the resistance of one part of the patient's mind and in a therapeutic alliance with another.

Group-analytic psychotherapy similarly attempts access to the unconscious defense struggle of each patient within the group by interpreting the ramifications of this defense struggle as they appear in verbal and nonverbal manifestations of group interaction. A basic reorganization of personality results when this attempt is successful. A climate is established for self-revelation in the course of which feedback (including inquiry and interpretation) from other group members as well as the conductor yields a gain in insight. It is this cycle that promotes personality change.

Siegmund Heinrich Foulkes (1948), the pioneer in group-analytic psychotherapy, pointed out some preliminary assumptions about it, summarized later in a lecture before the New York Academy of Medicine in 1958:

Firstly, that the character of any situation which we cultivate determines what goes on and what it means. *Secondly,* an assumption, based on universal observations regarding the behaviour of human beings brought together: they react, they show interest in each other and make contact. Thus they begin to interact, communicate, and form relationships. The processes just named are mutually interdependent and form a feedback system; in a way we may consider them as two triads of such a system: the first: reaction, interest, contact; the second: interaction, communication, relationship. *Thirdly*, we assume that modification of the group and of the individual are interdependent. Any change, any modification in the group, goes together with a change in the individual and vice versa. It follows that if we treat the group, we treat at the same time the individuals composing it, even if we do not apply ourselves to them in particular. *Fourthly*, we count on the inevitable repetition in transference, that is to say a displacement of old reactions into the treatment situation.

It is with these assumptions, amplified by the background of psychoanalytic knowledge and experience gained in two-person work, that we approach our task of reaching unconscious defenses and drives. For this purpose we create a group situation for free and spontaneous interaction and a wide range of communication. We want to create conditions which permit pathogenic conflicts to be verbally—and with increasing clarity—expressed within the group situation and to be worked-through in successive sessions. And we want to initiate at the same time a self-perpetuating process of revision so that our patients may acquire insight into the nature of their experiences and behavior.

Historically, group-analytic psychotherapy is rooted in both group psychotherapy and psychoanalysis. It is often said that modern group psychotherapy started in 1906 with J. H. Pratt's method (1907) of "mass instruction" for tubercular patients, but at that time Pratt was concerned with teaching groups of indigent consumptives about the need for a regimen of adequate rest, ample fresh air, and a varied and balanced diet. It was actually a quarter of a century later, as Corsini (1955) points out, that Pratt began planned group psychotherapy, this time not with individuals suffering frank physical disease, but with patients whose hypochondriacal complaints were unsupported by physical evidence. Long before this, J. L. Moreno (1923) had initiated his psychodramatic techniques in Vienna, and in 1932 he introduced the term "group psychotherapy", later (1947) establishing the first journal devoted to this activity.*

Edward W. Lazell (1921), Trigant Burrow (1927), L. C. Marsh (1935), Paul Schilder (1936), Louis Wender (1936), S. R. Slavson (1940), Samuel B. Hadden (1944), and J. W. Klapman (1959) were early pioneers of group psychotherapy in the United States, and their work took an analytic cast. An approach to analytic group psychotherapy had, however, already been implicit in the work of some psychotherapists usually considered to be exclusively interested in the individual. Conspicuous among these was Alfred Adler (1917), who, at a child guidance clinic in Vienna, often arranged for the teacher, the parents, the siblings, and even collaterals, as well as the young patient himself, to be present during the discussion of the patient's problems. Such sessions followed an initial individual exploration, but sometimes the group discussion that ensued dealt with the difficulties of those in contact with the child. During the 1920's, Rudolf Dreikurs (1951), a follower of Adler in the United States, developed a group approach based on Adlerian principles. All these therapeutic activities initiated the study of family dynamics, and ultimately led to the use of family therapy as a diagnostic tool and as a method of treating schizophrenic patients (Wynne et al., 1958; Bowen et al., 1959; Lidz, 1963). Therapy of these "natural" groups must be distinguished from group-analytic psychotherapy *per se*, and it should also be noted that Adler did not put the group, with its social interactional network, into the center of his method, although his theories indicate his high degree of sensitivity to social forces. His disciple, Joshua Bierer (Bierer and Haldane, 1941), later introduced group psychotherapy in the mental hospitals of the United Kingdom; he pioneered the therapeutic plan of using the hospital only by day, supplementing this type of hospitalization by what the neighboring community was encouraged to provide, especially in the establishment of "therapeutic clubs". His methods have been utilized widely in the context of the social emphasis now given in

* *Group Psychotherapy*, the official organ of the American Society of Group Psychotherapy and Psychodrama, published quarterly by Beacon House, Inc., New York.

the United Kingdom to the practice of psychiatry. One development of this trend is the "therapeutic community", the concept of which was first clearly detailed by T. F. Maine (1946) and elaborated by Maxwell Jones (1953).

It was also in the twenties that Foulkes read two papers by the American psychoanalyst and research psychiatrist, Trigant Burrow (1927, 1928). Burrow reported an extension of psychoanalysis by means of a group technique, in an application of his conjecture that the analysis of the individual could not be brought to completion without the opportunity of working-through social resistances in a group. (Incidentally, this proposition remains worthy of continued consideration in view of the disruptive behavior analyzed psychoanalysts themselves often bring to group situations.*) Burrow's later studies of tensions within groups, demonstrable in measurable physiological parameters, led him to posit further that these tensions were an expression of human phylic aberration which causes the individual to be uneasy—sometimes desperately so—and defensively concerned with his own identity when he is confronted by others. Burrow's views stimulated Foulkes to consider the possibility of group analysis as a means of treatment. Foulkes was also influenced by experiments in the drama then appearing on the stage. These bridges between the scientific and intuitive approach to meaning and identity formation will be dealt with in some detail in later chapters. Suffice it to say here that Foulkes (1964) acknowledges:

> There were other influences in the air at that time: apart from plays like *Six Characters in Search of an Author* by Pirandello, I remember being greatly impressed by Maxim Gorki's *The Lower Depths*. . . . Here was a play without a hero, a leaderless group on the stage, driven by strong, anonymous forces. I pondered about the pathogenic and therapeutic power of the

* Günter Ammon (1971) reports that the German Academy for Psychoanalysis (Deutsche Akademie für Psychoanalyse) now requires a preliminary year of analytic group therapy before an applicant is admitted for psychoanalytic training. The D.A.P. now requires 200 hours of training group analysis as well as at least 300 hours of later individual (training) analysis. Furthermore, the staff of the Training Institute of the German Academy for Psychoanalysis, Berlin, meets once a week for a group dynamic session to recognize and work through operative dynamics within their group.

theatre and of everyday life. . . . Fifteen years elapsed between this first germinal inception and my first actual experience with a group.

We have to take briefly into account the extraordinary influence in the thirties of Wilhem Reich (Ilse Reich, 1969) on many of the younger psychoanalysts, especially in Scandinavia after the publication of his *Massenpsychologie des Faschismus* in 1933 in Copenhagen. Reich invented the term *Sexual-Politik* (sex-politics) to refer to his development of the concept that the regulations within human society are related as much to the conscious and unconscious demands of sexual drives, especially to their distorted expression in political public life, as to socio-economic forces. The further development of this important concept, however, became embroiled in an essentially irrational turn of theory known as "Orgonomic Medicine". Nonetheless, a group approach based on Reich's immediately pre-orgone theory was developed in Oslo in association with the Nic Waal Institute. Today, 15 years after Reich's death in the Federal Penitentiary at Lewisburg, Pennsylvania, following the kind of bureaucratic stupidity (the emotional plague) he so much deplored, seeing–feeling–touching–experiencing encounter groups are applying—or misapplying unwittingly and recklessly—some of his ideas. The discarding of character armor to afford sexual and emotional release and to reconcile man and nature is now a leit-motif of these popular gatherings.

II Selection and Grouping

IN general, group-analytic therapy has been concerned with the treatment of psychoneurotic patients. It includes some of those with symptom neuroses but is more especially concerned with those who, while without frank symptoms of a hysterical, phobic, ruminative, or compulsive kind, are the victims of character neuroses that impair their interpersonal relations, mar their experience of marriage and parenthood, and lead to loneliness and withdrawal, feelings of failure, and general dissatisfaction or periodic depression. Persons with overt anxiety, conversion reactions, phobias, obsessions, or compulsive rituals, or with mixtures of these, also suffer from similar difficulties hidden beside or behind the clamor of their presenting symptoms.

Experience with group-analytic psychotherapy parallels that within the type of group psychotherapy described by Jerome D. Frank (1954), who felt that the selection of participants in a group of from five to eight persons presents certain difficult problems. He indicated the incompatibility of neurotics with alcoholic, psychopathic, or severely psychotic patients, but noted that ambulatory psychotics sometimes work along well with neurotic patients. He felt it inadvisable to introduce patients ashamed of their problems (homosexuals, for example) into the group not generally so characterized, and he reported that the advantage of having both sexes outweighs any initial difficulty presented by this mix.

One borderline or ambulatory schizophrenic patient may stimulate a group otherwise composed of psychoneurotic patients. However, such stimulation may be or become supra-maximal and create "condenser phenomena" (*vide infra*), be difficult to handle, and occasion acting-out outside of group therapy sessions. Unless the therapist has had considerable experience in group-analytic psychotherapy he is well advised to screen out from a group of neurotic patients those who have pronounced psychotic mechanisms. For such a group the goal is a balance between people with overtly similar or contrasting problems, dynamically related, and those whose difficulties are quite unrelated. The latter make possible greater clarity in the discerning of transference distortions.

A group-centered selection of members—a process in which the group's needs come first—favors the smooth development of the therapeutic process. This usually requires patients not too disparate in education, intelligence, and socio-economic status and background. A consciousness of kind promotes group cohesion and the mutual support which the group will surely need for an effective level of empathy. Guilt and anxiety reactions appearing concurrently with emotional release can be attenuated productively only in an empathic climate. Adequate motivation is important, since uncovering therapy demands a comparatively high degree of cooperation. Moreover, good intelligence, the capacity to verbalize, and the ability to attend sessions over a lengthy period are important considerations in the selection of group-analytic group members.

The reactions of the group conductor himself are also important; he is not making a selection of members for an abstract group-therapy group, but for *his* group, one which he will conduct and in which his approach and personality are of decisive importance.

In summary, the ideal group is one in which members are sufficiently alike to support one another, and yet different enough to expose each other to the stimulating effect of a wide variety of issues and ways of dealing with them. The remarks of F. B. Powdermaker and J. D. Frank (1953) about group psychotherapy in general remain applicable:

> It is usually desirable to have more than one representative of any particular outspoken trait, ethnic group or station in life. Each patient needs to perceive someone as a potential ally or at least as an equal. One college graduate in a group of workers, or one woman in a group of men, for example, is apt to feel isolated. One timid person in a group of talkers will feel hopelessly out of it, whereas two can exchange consoling glances.

Conversely, an aggressive talker will monopolize a group of timid patients to his and their disadvantage, but two or more will tend to hold each other in check.

Slavson (1964) has emphasized that an effort should be made to keep the range of patients' ego strengths and defenses within limits when grouping patients together for analytic work, lest a poorly compensated schizophrenic whose defenses are fragile slow down the pace of defense analysis in an analytic group—or sustain a psychotic break. The inclusion of such a patient in a group-analytic group in which the other patients have good ego strength but neurotic problems, and the necessity of conducting the group in consideration of the intrapsychic stress that he can stand without harm, may deprive the group as a whole of adequate therapy. Moreover, an outstandingly weak and disparate link in the chain would demand excessive individual attention from the conductor at the expense of collective therapy through or by the group itself. If the conductor concentrates too much on one member without regard to the therapeutic needs of the group as a whole, the patients outside the therapeutic orbit become resentful and increasingly resistive; disruption may then ensue before analytic work adequate to deal with hostile transference can sustain the group-analytic situation.

As already noted, Frank found it generally inadvisable to combine neurotic patients in group therapy with those who were alcoholic, severely psychotic, or sociopathic. This view agrees phenomenologically with the opinion expressed more dynamically by Slavson to the effect that patients in these three categories have gross ego deficiencies and weakness, and sometimes extremely brittle defenses. Further, the grossly manipulative and exploitative maladaptation of the sociopath is likely to waste too much of a group's time and energy for useful analytic therapy.

It is sometimes possible to introduce one patient from the classifications of more severe disturbance into a group composed of neurotic and borderline individuals without reducing its potential, but it is more customary to exclude them. They may, however, benefit from specialized methods of group therapy in a homogeneous matrix. Group therapy has proved serviceable in institutions for drug addicts, alcoholics, and delinquents, for example, and has even yielded benefits in homes for mental defectives. In these instances the methods used, although derived in part from psychoanalysis, depart from those employed in group-analytic psychotherapy with neurotics.

In studying dropouts from group therapy Irving D. Yalom (1966) found that few who had participated in less than 13 sessions had received even minimum benefit, and that their early departure threatened and sometimes demoralized those who remained in treatment in their respective groups. The success of analytic work in a group is favored by membership stability, and may be impeded by enrolling those likely to terminate prematurely, so early screening of such patients is advisable. Among the candidates for analytical group therapy who are usually unsuitable are those with consolidated defenses of denial and repression and a deemphasis of intrapsychic conflict or interpersonal disturbance, especially when they tend to attribute depressive problems wholly to bodily disease and/or external stress. When the preliminary psychiatric interview discloses the absence of "psychological-mindedness", group-analytic psychotherapy is contraindicated. Such persons may benefit, however, from slow analytic work in a predominantly supportive type of group psychotherapy that offers a less challenging situation.

As will be apparent from these clinical notes on selection and grouping, there is a need for further investigation in this area to refine our knowledge of the effectiveness of group-analytic psychotherapy. To what extent does the composition of the group (including the conductor) in respect to age, sex, clinical categories of disease, and personality typology affect outcome? Are not the experience, training, and personality of the conductor of major importance? On the one hand, it is undeniable that the therapist becomes the dominant transference target within the group; on the other hand, timely transference interpretation provides the most powerful therapeutic leverage.

III Initiating Therapy

WHEN diagnostic evaluation has admitted a potential group member, an interview should then prepare him for the group sessions. He should be briefly informed about the purposes and general *modus operandi* of the therapeutic group, and led to see that his complaints and interpersonal problems may be connected with emotional difficulties and mental conflicts. The group may then be described as a means whereby he may be able to work out and understand some of his emotional problems and at least to increase his understanding of others in the therapeutic alliance. The permissive nature of the proceedings and the confidentiality of group discussion should be emphasized in the preparatory interview.

Early meetings disclose the means each patient uses to gain a feeling of security in the group and to claim the attention of its conductor. The conscious and unconscious social roles that have disturbed the relationships of each member with others become apparent through these efforts. Important clues to underlying conflicts and habitual ways of dealing with them may thus become available. The therapist should pay little attention to lengthy discussion of symptoms, and should refrain from offering advice and lecturing on such topics as the relationship between bodily disturbance and emotional problems. He should, however, listen attentively to spontaneous accounts of the history and current situation of any patient. Members are encouraged to get acquainted with one another. This encouragement should be deft, with the therapist only minimally active in the process.

Foulkes (1948) indicated that although the therapist owes the group an opening explanation of its procedures, his words are secondary to his adroit establishment and management of an appropriate situation. Spontaneity is important for him as well as for the others, but he may introduce group members and ask each in turn to reveal his complaints, what he believes to have caused them, and what he regards as a possible remedy. Although the ensuing free-style exchange may be supported by the therapist, it is expected to develop around these disclosures rather than to adhere to any stated rule. The protocol, which may be formally articulated at the outset, emphasizes free participation and a ready flow of topics, without the orderliness of a discussion in which only sequential or clearly relevant contributions are welcome.

Whether he expresses the goals or not, the conductor establishes early acceptance of this kind of exchange by helping members to appreciate the significance of even apparently inconsequential utterances, and to become aware of anything that obstructs spontaneous expression. The basic rule of group-analytic therapy alluded to here is: Talk about anything that comes to mind, without selection. Expression in the group situation differs from that in the dyadic situation of individual analysis, just as in analysis it differs from that in attempted self-analysis. "Free association" is in no way independent of the total situation. Foulkes describes its appearance in the group as "free-floating discussion".

The conductor avoids lectures, exhortations, advice, and explanations as much as possible, since these only too often serve the patient's resistances and give him excuses to escape from facing his underlying emotional problems. If, however, the patient is brought into a situation which he himself is continuously helping to create, he is forced to come out into the open with his own reactions and their contradictory aspects. He meets himself in the situation and projects his own personality and fantasies into it. He cannot escape it, nor can he help facing the others and their problems, seeing himself as in a mirror. Foulkes (1948) calls for a minimum of program and a maximum of free self-expression and participation, noting that the less closely defined the possibilities are the more the patient must stretch and invest himself in the performance.

In initial group sessions some patients persist in voicing wonder about what they are supposed to do. This is apt to occur especially when a recounting of their symptoms no longer elicits much if any interest. Often this reiteration occurs despite the examples set by other patients who have already started to discuss their respective situations in life, including their feelings, and the development of these situations, especially their problematic aspects. These other patients have already noted from the interest of the conductor and his other reactions—including, notably, his verbalized attempts at understanding—that these kinds of communication are preferred. Patients who maintain that they are nonplussed are, of course, resistive, either consciously or unconsciously, to sharing their intimate experiences with others in the group at this time. The conductor may then explain that it is only when members tell more about themselves that the efforts of the others to understand them can begin to bear fruit. Some patients respond with a summary story of their lives, and sometimes through a question or two some aspects of the more emotionally charged portions of this story are elicited, first perhaps by the conductor but shortly by other group members. In this pre-analytic phase of exploratory contact seeking, the issue of confidentiality arises conspicuously, although it had been touched upon earlier. Gradually the group-analytic situation becomes clearer and an analytic contract is established. The terms of the contract become further clarified as occasion indicates or necessitates—that is, through the scrutiny of spontaneously occurring incidents. The terms are that the members of the group are expected to reveal themselves, their inner biographies, what is important to them now, what was of importance to them, or seemed to be, and their plans, their hopes, and their fears. And they are expected to try to understand each other, communicating verbally, and rigorously respecting the rule that all communications in the group are to be treated as altogether confidential.

The conductor, of course, is aware of the difficulties involved in adherence to the rules, and knows that the patients will, in fact, use all kinds of defensive evasions. Moreover, in this era of encounter groups, explicit attention may need to be given to the analytic rule that physical contact between members is not compatible with a therapeutic method which is essentially a "talking cure". A crucial aspect of the group's work is the analysis of resistance, and this can be accomplished only in the absence of an acting-out of erotic and hostile impulses. The analytic atmosphere and the analytic work would both be wrecked were this acting-out to be permitted. Just as psychoanalysis has a rigid framework within which the freedom of verbal expression is permitted and encouraged, so does group-analytic psychotherapy have a framework, different only insofar as differences are determined by the number of people physically present.

The discovery that the group and its conductor accept past actions which have heretofore earned disapproval or severe punishment reduces guilty feelings and provides a corrective experience. At the same time, friendly but critical responses eventually impress upon the patient the desirability of examining the background of his acting-out, which is so often self-defeating or self-debasing in the long—if not also in the short—run.

A significant tendency toward solidarity and common response to the analyst soon develops within the group. Libidinal attachments lead members to help the therapist and to try to understand one another in ways useful for therapy. Through their interaction efforts to overcome individual resistances are made, and these often lead speedily to some improvement, allowing the analyst to concentrate on resistance and problems that are common. Group treatment can offer initial advantages to the therapist, who will, however, often find that greater effort than that required in individual analysis is subsequently demanded of him.

Without further comment on the initiation of the therapeutic process in a group setting, it will be apparent that the conductor should largely avoid obstructing the healing forces released within the group and should instead let the group act as an instrument for therapeutic advantage. However, a strongly authoritarian personality in the conductor, his own excessive need for appreciation, any unsatisfactory peer relationships he may have, or some other personal problem may make this very hard for him indeed; in his reactions to the group he may obstruct the initiation of the analytic therapeutic process. Insofar as his ego founders on his id the group process is endangered. Many things can happen then, including group disruption or a wasteful and disappointing use of time.

In group-analytic psychotherapy the conductor promotes the interaction of the group members, and it is this which initiates the therapeutic process. He observes and deals with the same forces in the group situation as in individual analysis—unconscious drives, conscience reactions, and adaptations to reality. However, these forces display themselves in a different balance from that seen in individual psychotherapy. In the group setting the impact with concrete social reality is more conspicuous, whereas this is often in the background in the dyadic setting. As Nathan W. Ackerman (1945) wrote:

> In a group situation, adaptation to social reality is a constantly changing observable phenomenon. The immediate social reality is a fluid one because it is variously personified by one patient or another, the group as a whole, or by the therapist.

Concepts specific to group analysis and essential for understanding the group-analytic process have been evolved by Foulkes and others, reflecting the fact that this emphasis is different from that in individual psychoanalysis.

IV Micro-sociology of the Small Therapy Group

MIRROR reactions typically appear when a number of persons meet and interact. A person sees himself or part of himself—often a repressed part—dramatically reflected in the interactions of other group members. He may see his neighbors reacting in the way he does himself, or in contrast to his own overt behavior. A patient may identify with another member's characteristic traits or responses, regarding them as more effective than his own; in this case, he will turn to that fellow member as a "positive role model". He may, however, see in the conduct of another a caricature of his own and come to realize why his own responses have been ineffective or have antagonized others; the fellow member he watches with such insight will then serve as a "negative role model".

In group-analytic psychotherapy he also gets to know about himself from the way others describe him. Thus there is a revisiting and revising of a fundamental process in ego development through this immediate experience of his effect on others and of the discussion of the pictures of him that they form and convey.

The *occupation* of the therapy group differs from that of the ordinary group convened for work or play. There is no manifest, deliberately agreed-upon occupation apart from psychotherapy, although one may adventitiously appear as a defense against intimate, interpersonal reactions and thoughts. This defensive or screen function makes the concept of "occupation" important for the understanding of group dynamics.

In contrast to group-analytic psychotherapy, some forms of group therapy utilize nonverbal occupations to secure group cohesion and to induce mutual support and cooperation. A small group of patients may be given a house to build or farm labor to perform, for example; such projects can be part and parcel of the repressive-inspirational approach, and can be immensely beneficial for some patients. Certain kinds of occupation especially conducive to emotional release, such as work together in music, painting, or dancing, may be followed by discussions aimed at understanding and integrating the esthetic experience. Aimée Baruch (1969) notes:

> Art therapy is one of the means by which a reservoir of the unconscious can be reached. When people are asked to draw pictures at first they are bewildered. What does one do without words? They generally go back to infancy, when the world was a series of pictures thrown on a sensitive screen. This may indicate why the first art therapy session begins with a great many "womb" pictures. In subsequent sessions other early memories are also expressed on paper. Alfred Adler's conviction that the child's earliest memory is significant for his whole life has been confirmed, and is of great help to me in my work.

Some patients may require nonverbal exercises to undercut their consolidated defenses, or they may be excluded from group-analytic psychotherapy proper by their poorly developed verbal facility. It is to be borne in mind that there are several roads to Rome, and that some offer more interest and advantage to some people than others do. As stated, there is, however no such manifest occupation within the framework of group-analytic psychotherapy, and this relative abstention from motor activity puts an immediate emphasis on verbal expression. There is a considerable therapeutic advantage in containing feelings and fantasies on a verbal level when this is at all basically possible; in group-analytic psychotherapy defense against this possibility needs careful scrutiny.

Scapegoatism often develops promptly out of the group's need to project accumulated feelings of guilt. Quite early in the therapeutic process a scapegoat may be identified, sometimes in an effort to deal with emergent ambivalent and guilty feelings about the conductor. These guilty feelings are genetically determined by problematic filial conflicts which are also often enmeshed with sibling rivalries. The scapegoat is often one of the group members who invites this position, driven by an unconscious need for punishment. An attempted "riddance of evil" may later become temporarily focused on the group conductor during the middle phase of group-analytic psychotherapy in a reminder of the periodic expulsion of a divine King as scapegoat in primitive society, elucidated by Géza Rohéim (1920) many years ago.

The conductor should understand the concept of *resonance* and recognize the ways in which messages each member receives within the group are unconsciously weighted with reference to the psycho-sexual developmental level at which the hearer is "set". For example, mention of cattle grazing in a field might activate one member to an expression reflective of his infantile experiences of breast feeding; evoke fear in another about possible mutilation of his body; and lead a third to ruminations (*sic*) on his economic situation or the exorbitant price of beef.

The term *condenser phenomenon* is used to describe the sudden discharge of deep and primitive material following the pooling of associated ideas within the group. The members' interactions may suddenly loosen group resistances and cause a surprising eruption of common group fears or fantasies. The surprise comes from the absence of apparent, conscious causal relationships; the hidden parameter is the charging of common repressed unconscious fantasies. For example, this charging may be activated by one member's dream recital that occasions massive group resonance connected perhaps with preceding events in the group.

Jonathan Guttmacher and Lee Birk (1971) have noted that there are people who say little in the therapy group but who obviously are quite intently absorbed in what is going on. After some months in therapy they will report major changes in their lives outside the group. Thus sometimes patients in groups may improve dramatically through work that is to a large extent silent and out of view, in what Guttmacher and Birk label the *iceberg phenomenon*. On the other hand, some very sick patients appear to make great strides within the therapy group, forming meaningful object relationships for the first time. After several years they come to show greater openness and trust, and to exhibit empathy with other group members. They cope better when confronted by stresses within the group such as the eruption of open anger, the disclosure of sexual feelings, or the termination of fellow members, but in their lives outside the group they change at a much slower pace, and in a way that is almost the antithesis of the sudden dramatic improvement of the iceberg phenomenon. Guttmacher and Birk report:

> Within the group one chronic schizophrenic man is a very real and valued member, but outside to a large extent he remains isolated. His out-of-group friendships have slowly increased in number and depth but at an almost agonizingly slow pace. He has now been able to go back to school successfully, but this took several years to accomplish and was accompanied by many crises. Within the group his genuine feelings, insight, and concern for others are typically very impressive. But the expression of these feelings outside the protected setting of the group had been quite difficult, and what has been accomplished outside the group has been done at an extremely slow pace especially compared to the two women patients cited as examples of the iceberg phenomenon.

Early in the therapeutic process group members may unconsciously cast the conductor in the role of an omniscient and omnipotent leader, expect magical help, and experience rage or other shared reactions if this expectation is disappointed. This state of affairs often accounts for the early display of phenomena which some of the concepts just outlined help one to understand and to deal with by translation into the common group wishes, fears, and defenses.

The scale of observation for the therapist in group therapy is shifted from that in individual treatment. He has another frame of reference here, one of different emphasis. This requires of him the observational stance for which his psychoanalytic understanding should provide a particularly good preparation—that of the micro-sociologist. However, there are many who have psychoanalytic training or who have undergone individual analysis as part of their professional training who are singularly inept in the group setting. For these a personal experience of group-analytic psychotherapy is necessary before they attempt to serve as conductor of a group. Such experience usually contributes also to their more effective behavior in groups in general.

The conductor's function in group-analytic therapy is to use the group as an instrument for therapy, and this aim determines his behavior from the beginning. The medium through which he works is verbal communication which can be understood and shared by all. For this to be effective he must take into account the situation of the whole group as well as the possible effect on any one of its members. This awareness may at times be particularly important in respect to the interpretation of a member's communication which is superficially, but not at a deeper level, unrelated to ongoing group events. Moreover, it is well to recall that Foulkes contrasted the procedures used in individual and group psychotherapy in respect to providing interpretations; he indicated that whereas in the former the therapist often voices interpretation, the group conductor tries to elicit them from the group. Observations and interpretations of peers often convey greater impact than those offered by the conductor, especially in the case of those patients whose social behavior requires challenge before they can begin to recognize that they subvert their own social goals. Often, too, the conductor is required to sustain a quietly supportive role when a member is enduring criticisms or struggling with peer interpretations.

To avoid the group's being led in the usual sense, the group conductor's activity should be characterized by a discrimination different from that required in individual therapy, although in either role he remains in the background, benevolently neutral, and disengages himself as far as possible. It is remarkable how difficult many people confronted by a group find this. The discipline of subordinating one's own interests to the patient's interest is a cardinal principle of psychiatric work in general, and analytic psychotherapy in particular. Lengthy experience has led me to believe that for many people this subordination of self is not possible in group therapy without considerable specific training beyond that required for psychoanalysis itself. We certainly need to understand more about the temptations of the therapy group, which is a captive audience *par excellence*.

There are two related sets of problems which recurrently arise with neophyte therapists, most of whom, however, surmount them in training. Other psychotherapists are ultimately eliminated as group conductors one way or another by the groups they attempt to conduct; the analytic process is wrecked under their direction in any case. The first counter-transference problem relates to excessive efforts the therapist might intrusively make to build himself up, to mop up the admiration of the group, or to inspire awe. Such inappropriate efforts are related to narcissistic injuries and flaws within himself centered around unresolved exhibitionistic-modesty conflicts. The second problem relates to an excessive identification with the aggressive father as a defense against anxiety about being overpowered or overwhelmed by the group; this is centered around unresolved sadomasochistic conflicts.

V Group-analytic Psychotherapy, Group Therapy, and the "Therapeutic Community"

THE treatment of sickness by inspiration and suggestion is described in the records of ancient history, as in those of the Greek priest-physicians who offer many examples in their temple practice of the healing art. The primitive witch doctor, whose practices antedate recorded history, still continues in some parts of the world to affect susceptibility to disease and recovery from it by the rites he performs.

Franz Anton Mesmer may be cited as a conspicuous link between the magical and religious methods of treatment and modern psychotherapy. Stefan Zweig (1933) describes Mesmer's Paris clinic in 1780:

> The windows were screened by curtains so that no more than a dim twilight should pervade the place; thick carpets, and hangings on the walls, deadened every sound; mirrors were so placed as to reflect a golden light; while strange astronomical signs were introduced to attract attention and at the same time to leave the mind unsatisfied. The indefinable always enhances expectation, mystery gives rise to tension, silence and secrecy stimulate the emotions. Hence in Mesmer's room every sense—those of sight, of hearing, of touch—was titillated in the most delicate way in order to produce a combined effect of soothing and stimulation. Like a great pool, the healing tub, the famous baquet, stood in the middle of the room. As in a church, silence prevailed, and the sick would gather breathlessly expectant around the magnetic altar.

There the patients heard music playing softly as attendants arranged them in a human chain around the baquet which contained iron filings immersed in water. Rods of iron projected from the tub, and the patients applied the distal ends to ailing parts of the body as they were directed to do. Mesmer himself then appeared in a colorful robe of lilac silk, a long iron wand in his hand. At that time he believed that an impalpable fluid saturated with "animal magnetism" could be manipulated by his will and, augmented by mineral magnetism, could cure his patients. Zweig writes about this:

Usually no great time elapsed before one or other of the company would begin to tremble, then the limbs would start to twitch convulsively, and the patient would break out in perspiration, would scream or groan. No sooner had such tokens manifested themselves in one member of the chain, than the others, too, would feel the onset of the famous crisis which was to bring relief.... One need but study contemporary woodcuts to learn the kind of reactions the patient underwent... meanwhile the strains of music continued to be wafted from a neighbouring room in order to create an even tenser situation—for according to Mesmer's theory of crises the malady had to be provoked into its utmost marge of development, it had so to speak to be sweated out of the organism if the body was to regain health. Those in whom the crisis was very violent were carried into the "salle des crises" in order that composure might gradually be restored; and the comic-papers of the day did not lose an opportunity of hinting that the ladies were restored by highly physiological means. The most extraordinary scenes were daily enacted in Mesmer's magnetic room; a man would spring up and away from the baquet, thereby breaking the magnetic chain, and would declare himself cured; another would cast himself at Mesmer's feet and kiss the master's hands; others would beseech him to increase the force of the magnetic current, or would beg him to touch them once again.

It is clear that the prompt removal of symptoms of some few patients and the ecstatic or convulsive crises of others greatly impressed the rest and escalated therapeutic events within the group. For a time Mesmer enjoyed ever-increasing professional prestige among the powerful and wealthy of Paris, as well as the learned; this powerfully affected the success of his work with any particular single patient in an individual séance. However, as resistance to the master and his methods developed, the rationalizations by which Mesmer and others had explained his treatment were abandoned, and he later found it necessary to leave the scene of his medical triumphs.

This highly abridged account of Mesmer's work emphasizes the fact that personal and institutional charisma is always a product of group interaction, and inseparable also ultimately from individual (two-person) psychotherapy that uses inspiration and suggestion. Though Mesmer had not developed an adequate theoretical grasp of the nature of suggestion, his "scientific" opponents were in worse shape intellectually. It took almost a century for the French Academy, at Charcot's insistence, to recognize hypnotism officially. As Zweig writes:

> A wrong-headed decision taken by the academic bodies in the case of Franz Anton Mesmer had delayed this recognition for a whole century when, with a trifle more clarity of mind and application, science might already have been enriched with the new acquisition as early as 1784.

One should note here that not only is the power of suggestion heightened under certain conditions of group interaction but that, paradoxically, its presence under group conditions may be difficult to identify—subtle, and often elusive.

Mesmer's conviction of the saturation of an impalpable fluid with animal magnetism is a not altogether misplaced metaphoric approximation of the truth, however false it may be in literal terms.* The concept of suggestion was limited in the eighteenth century, much more severely limited than it need be today after Freud's epoch-making psychoanalytic work. Mesmer's magnetic fluid, regarded as analogy or metaphor, recognizes the existence of a certain class

* We note the same confusion of metaphor and reality in Wilhelm Reich's later theory building which included the Orgone. In Reich's case, however, there is more general evidence of the progressive encroachment of a tragic mental derangement besides the beginnings of regressive disorder of metaphoric symbolism, whereas Mesmer was simply unable to reach beyond the fashionable semantic physical environment of the medical epoch of the Enlightenment. See *Speech and reason* (Abse, 1971).

of phenomena and permits a glimpse of their nature. Such considerations as these suggest that Pratt's teaching of a group of tubercular patients, although based on his knowledge of physical ways to enhance the body's resistance to disease, was also attended by a cirumfluent aura of suggestion and inspiration. Despite Corsini's rider (see page 5) we are obliged to think of it as group-inspirational psychotherapy, although it was not planned as such. His later *planned* group psychotherapy for neurotic hypochondriacal patients was based partly on his own experience and subsequent recognition of this psychotherapeutic element, a recognition which may have come about through his association with two psychologically sophisticated clergymen concerned with the healing ministry of the church.

It might have been expected that demonstrations of the frequent modifications of both organic disease (tuberculosis) and neurotic disability by inspirational and suggestive methods of group psychotherapy would lead to the testing of planned group psychotherapy for the relief of many disorders now described as "psychosomatic". This has actually occurred only rarely; instances will be cited. On the contrary, most psychosomatic reactors find themselves in general hospitals when they become sick enough. There they undergo intensive and extensive physical investigation and receive physical treatment accompanied by little or no planned psychotherapy of any kind. Unfortunately, they may find themselves in a situation which is decidedly anti-therapeutic in important psychological aspects—impersonal, and influenced by the present emphasis on laboratory techniques, computerized diagnosis, bureaucratic management by non-physicians, and nursing personnel trained away from personal patient care.

In the psychiatric wards of the general hospital, however, the patient usually finds himself in a milieu that takes into account the value of the "therapeutic community" and its considerable contribution to patient care and recovery. The therapeutic elements in a community are often amplified through large-group meetings and sometimes further enhanced by small-group therapy sessions. It is beyond our present purpose to discuss fully here the application of psychoanalytic principles to hospital inpatient care, but the effects of group therapy influenced by psychoanalytic knowledge may be briefly illustrated.

Small groups composed of inpatients who are schizophrenic or depressed often respond favorably to group psychotherapy given concomitantly with pharmacotherapy, or after shock therapy has been administered. This small group provides a particularly useful way-station for many patients when they are reaching out once more for contact with others but are still anxious about any social situation too far removed from the doctor–nurse–patient nexus. The group therapist must usually become immediately active in reducing anxiety and explaining the purpose of the group sessions. It has been my experience that these sessions are most successful when the first focus is on the current problems of the patients, especially their feelings about being in the hospital and about leaving it in the care of their relatives, and about the treatment they have received. The group responds to a repressive-inspirational type of group therapy when this permits adequate ventilation of complaints and is open to an investigative approach to some important common problems. Thus such a group often approaches schizotypical problems about the excessive need for and the fear of support from hospital staff and relatives (Abse and Estes, 1952). Clarification of these problems in an empathic group climate is a powerful therapeutic maneuver. The self-esteem of these patients is often in jeopardy; they defend themselves by extravagant means against intense dependency longings. The therapist can apply his psychoanalytic knowledge to adjust the inspirational element to the continuing fundamental need for support. If, however, the therapist goes along blindly with the patients' unrealistic and distorted insistence on an excessive independence—possibly as part of his own unconscious reaction to their fundamentally primitive type of dependency need, or as part of his own misguiding "cultural superego"—the group situation would in the longer run become anti-therapeutic. The group therapy should be integrated with discussions with the nursing staff since patients become more self-assertive during the course of the group sessions. While working through their problems in an atmosphere of group support they may change on the ward from appreciative parasites to hostile contenders. Such a development often makes it clearly necessary to deal with the counter-transference reactions of nurses who all too easily come to feel that their patients' bones are filled, not with red marrow like their own, but with black ingratitude.

Group-analytic psychotherapy sprang historically from psychoanalysis and from supportive, didactic, and suggestive group psychotherapy. Many alert group therapists now use their understanding gained from experience in group-analytic psychotherapy in the more supportive forms of group therapy and in communication with the nursing staff, thus improving the more general therapeutic community of the ward. For example, a young married woman beginning remission from a schizophrenic break with reality finds the courage to discuss her wishes and fears about possibly returning to her husband, and her wishes and fears about possibly returning instead to her mother. A plan is evolved and animatedly discussed within the group; the suggestion is that she return to her husband, but remain near enough to her mother to see her at monthly intervals but not so near her that her regressive vulnerability and her mother's anachronistic continuation of mothering patterns inhibit her growing up. Such an example would, of course, be explored further in terms of the events in the group which reflected the useful externalization of her repressed inner conflicts of ambivalence.

Joseph Abrahams and Edith Varon (1953) in *Maternal dependency in schizophrenia* discuss their experience with analytic group therapy for young woman inpatients at St. Elizabeth's Hospital in Washington, D.C., and their visiting mothers. This two-year program, with seven pairs of mothers and patients, disclosed the mothers' emotional dependence on their daughters, who responded by a conspicuous current of cold rejection. The mothers frequently displayed an extremely condescending and destructive attitude of superiority toward their daughters, who acquiesced in a demonstration of their low self-esteem and infantile insecurity. These revelations of complex pathogenic mother–daughter relationships appeared in a group climate which promoted therapeutic intervention in a process which was perpetuating the schizophrenic disorder. Other examples illustrative of different facets of human relatedness could be offered, but this one amply demonstrates that common "schizophrenic" problems can be profitably dealt with in a setting of group support and interest which promotes insight, emotional release, and reality-testing.

It is true that group work with schizophrenics and depressives requires much effort and stamina on the part of the conductor; the constant possibility of group-disruptive hostilities requiring vigilance and redirection makes demands on the energy of the therapist. Even when the group work is conducted on a level which is predominantly one of support the patients will benefit from their enhanced potential of communication and reality-testing, as well as from those valuable occasional moments when ego-strengthening insights can be achieved in the group. Moreover, the investigative value of analytic group work is shown in the disclosure and exploration of common problems of schizoid and depressive personalities. Members of the nursing staff become better acquainted with the problems of their patients in the process, either through interaction with the conductor or the patient himself, or by participation in the group as an observer; such improved understanding often leads to better communication between nurses and doctors, and hence to an improved milieu for the patient.

A notable example of a total psychotherapeutic program of experiential interaction in this country is that devised and developed by Lorant Forizs and his associates at Tarpon Springs, Florida. Here each inpatient's treatment program consists of regular individual psychotherapy (usually thrice weekly) together with therapeutic experiences in a number of different groups. The superordinate responsibility for the patient is taken by the psychiatrist who conducts the individual psychotherapy. There are three ward or community groups, each of from 25 to 50 patients, responsible for planning activities for its own members. The proportion of the activities taking place inside the hospital building, outside on the hospital grounds, or in field trips to nearby cities, varies. Community group 1 is composed of the sickest patients who require, in general, more constant support and attention than do patients in the other two community groups. Their life centers around the hospital's intensive care unit, which is a round building with all rooms in full view of the nurses' station in the center. When these patients go into other areas of the hospital, or out into the gardens, they are accompanied by staff members, even when the activity is a recreational activity planned by the group as a whole.

Although its members assume few responsibilities on their own, the structure and working of this community group (C–1) are like those of the two others (C–2 and C–3). Each group elects its own leaders: a group chairman, vice-chairman, secretary, sergeant-at-arms; also a rules committee, food committee, and recreation, legal, and advisory committees. And, within the framework of hospital rules, each makes its own rules for its members to live by.

Each community group has a medical therapist who serves more as a catalyst than as an authority, occasionally suggesting a point that has been overlooked or opening up a new direction for the discussion to take. The group is concerned with almost all activities affecting the current lives of its members, discussing them sometimes before and sometimes after the occasion: for example, providing companions for a member in need of around-the-clock help for a few days, or a chaperone for another who needs to go to town to shop.

The hospital refrains from imposing rules except in matters of safety. By allowing each group to make, change, and enforce the rules for its own members it avoids the splitting of "establishment" and "the downtrodden".

The three community groups meet independently twice weekly for an hour and a half. Meetings are conducted under Robert's Rules of Order, with reports from committees, motions, records, discussion, and votes. Attendance at all meetings is expected of each patient. The doctor assigned to the groups attends, as do representatives from all the other departments of the hospital.

Most patients on first entering the hospital are assigned to community group C–2, whose members usually have the free run of the hospital and grounds, and may go beyond the grounds with a group of patients for a shopping or sightseeing trip.

Unless events make it necessary the staff continues its role as observer, or, when consulted, lets recommendations go back to the community group meeting for further discussion and decision. This encourages the community members to solve their own problems, and to gain experience in understanding those of others.

Members of a community group take care of one another, much as an older brother or sister might in a large family. For instance, one may oversee another while he shaves, wake another for breakfast, coerce still another into eating, or listen as one expresses anger at a doctor. Also like brothers and sisters in a family, community members tell about one another. The patient who has broken some rule is "on report", whether it is a hospital rule or one of the community group to which he belongs. At times the group seems much harder on a member who has committed an infraction than staff personnel would be. This discipline by their peers is much more effective than any that might have been imposed by the staff.

Community group 3 theoretically has the greatest latitude, in privileges as well as responsibilities. Members of this group have many out-of-the-hospital activities such as attendance at college classes, concerts, or theater parties. Some may even live outside the hospital in nearby communities while continuing their therapy and maintaining active membership in C–3. The staff comes to the assistance of members of C–3 when called upon, or when the situation warrants. In general, however, C–3 members get the message "You're on your own for the most part", and they are expected to be planning the life they want to have when they leave the hospital. This period of weaning can sometimes be too stressful and have regressive shifts which, if not weathered in the individual and small-group psychotherapies, may result in the patient's transfer to C–1 lest he become disruptive within C–3. The decision for such transfer rests with the patient's individual therapist.

New leaders are elected each month, new rules made, and a new cycle of community living begun; this "revolving responsibility" may be one of the main reasons for the group's usual effectiveness in giving its members useful experiences in getting along with other people. Group rules preclude the retaining of any set of leaders in office long enough to form a static governing body or to identify a powerful élite; the leader of one month becomes a follower the next, and although individuals may be assigned back and forth among the groups, the achievement goals of each remain constant.

Samuel B. Schiff and Sidney M. Glassman (1969) consider that there are two basic approaches to the large group—that of Maxwell Jones's (1953, 1966) attempt to induce "a living-learning experience" and that of Marshall Edelson (1964, 1967) who emphasizes its "socio-therapeutic function". Edelson sees community meetings as "task-orientated groups designed to examine and resolve conflicts which inhibit optimal organizational effectiveness". Within a strictly applied task orientation of this kind the expression and scrutiny of intrapsychic problems and conflicts are inhibited, and—so far as such material appears at all—the task is impeded. Large groups can of course be conducted so that the personal dynamics of some of the participants can also be approached while others are spectators in a role not without its learning and therapeutic aspects.

At the Anclote Psychiatric Center Forizs has continued the attempt to secure and integrate the best of all the worlds of psycho-therapeutic influence: individual analytically oriented psycho-therapy, the large-group approach, and the small therapy group. This requires open communication between the several therapists engaged in one mode or another with a particular patient, for this is a multiple therapy method. Necessary communication is secured through a daily round-table conference of therapists whose successive reports about individual patients are recorded as they are communicated, with the individual therapists entering into discussion following each report.

In 1948 Foulkes noted that "for the purpose of such highly intimate work as group analysis numbers cannot be large". He later (1964) acknowledged the value of ward meetings of 30 to 80 patients, but added: "More is needed, however. The patient needs insight . . . into his own conditions and life, insight into his present feelings, behavior and reaction. Therein lie the limitations of a large meeting. . . . For this a more intimate setting is essential: the small psychotherapeutic group."

Lionel Kreeger (1972) has recently said of group therapy in the institutional setting:

> I think that it is true that groups are essential to the working of a therapeutic community, but that a therapeutic community setting is not essential to the running of groups. Nevertheless, large groups or community meetings are a most important aspect of institutional organisation. What transpires in these large groups is determined firstly by the orientation of staff but secondly by the demands of the patient population. I can easily appreciate Edelson's clarification of the use of large groups in a setting in which patients will have the opportunity of exploring their own personal pathology in either individual psychotherapy or small group psychotherapy, or both. Under these circumstances, it is valid to restrict the functioning of the large group to socio-therapeutic ends. Where there is an absence or a severe limitation of individual and small group experience, however, the pressures within the large group may be directed towards obtaining personal growth and resolution of neurotic problems in the large group setting.

Actually, it remains doubtful whether resolution of neurotic problems can occur in such large-group settings when this is the only mode of therapy. Neurotic problems may, of course, temporarily subside and be to a considerable extent masked by active participation in large groups, especially those led by evangelical leaders.

VI The Development and Termination of the Group-analytic Situation

IN 1936, in a rare instance of planned group psychotherapy for psychosomatic reactors, M. N. Chappell, G. G. Stefano, G. S. Rogerson, and F. H. Pike gave group psychotherapy to patients with demonstrated peptic ulcers refractory to the usual medical treatment. Thirty-two such patients were given a six-week course of daily didactic group therapy which included explanations, advice about living patterns, and the promotion of "visceral rest". These workers demonstrated a better response to adjunctive didactic group therapy than the improvement achieved in a control group given the same medical regimen without any planned psychotherapy. At the end of three months 30 of the group patients were symptom-free; one could not be located, and one was only once again transiently beset with ulcer symptoms. The recurrence rate was much higher in the control group, in which 18 out of 20, after an initially good response to the medical regimen, had full recurrence in the period in question. At the end of three years 28 of the original group therapy patients were located and reexamined; 24 were without serious symptoms, and 15 of these were symptom-free, or almost so. Only two were as sick and apparently as subject to recurrences as they had been at the start of the study.

In considering the role of influence in psychotherapy, Jerome D. Frank (1961) compares the Chappell study with that performed by John Fortin and myself in 1956. Frank points out that the results of daily didactic group psychotherapy of six weeks' duration seemed to be as durable as, and more speedily attained than, the results of twice-weekly, one-and-a-half-hour sessions of group-analytic psychotherapy during the course of one year. Frank writes, "It appears as if patients reflected differences in the therapists' expectancies by the speed with which they improved." The difficulty with this conclusion is that I had no conscious special time expectancy nor did Fortin! However, it is to be conceded that we were much more interested in basic personality change than in the speed with which symptoms receded, and perhaps this circumstance may be considered as a weak support for Frank's simple explanation. As will be apparent, however, the whole course of events in analytic group therapy is different from and more complex than that of a covering type of therapy. Certainly, patients in analytic groups do have a tendency to swing more symptomatically, and sometimes phasically; sometimes, too, becoming worse symptomatically before they get better. This swing is a function of the derepressive dynamics of the processes of treatment, not simply a reflection of the therapist's expectations. Indeed, expectancy becomes realistically associated preconsciously with following the processes in therapy.

Dependency–independency conflicts were heightened during a second regressive phase of group-analytic psychotherapy with a group of ulcer patients when their ulcer symptoms actually recurred (Fortin and Abse, 1956). First, unrealistic expectations of help from the therapist were disappointed; resentment and attempts to take over leadership ensued. Hostile competition resulted, with a decrease in the alliance and cohesive support within the group in this second phase. Feelings that support, either from the conductor or from other group members, was lacking reawakened dependency strivings which, however, were conflicted; symptoms of an ulcer type again emerged. As stated, the members of Chappell's group were symptomatically getting better within this period of time, whereas those of Fortin's group were in pain. Fortin's peptic ulcer patients then dealt with their situation by the scapegoat device, whereupon mutual support became possible for all but one, and painful symptoms receded. Later, indeed, there was sufficient group cohesion and guilt reduction for "aggression-out" to be turned against the therapist in direct verbal attacks. The transference significances of these events became clearer, and when they were interpreted in the further course of therapy they periodically evoked pertinent memories of childhood that revealed the essence of the inner biography. Difficulties in the achievement of a more active masculine identification became evident and were gradually surmounted in the further course of treatment.

Thus it was possible to discern several overlapping phases in the group-analytic psychotherapy: an initial anxious phase marked by silences and demands for guidance by the therapist; a second phase of competition for individual leadership and rebellion against authority; a third phase, ushered in by scapegoatism and soon followed by open group hostility toward the therapist; a fourth phase of considerable discussion of personal problems, increasingly including productive introspective analytic work by the group members, a feature which persisted into and through the final phase of termination, with fluctuations.

This short résumé of the sequence of events during one year in which eight patients met twice weekly for one-and-a-half-hour sessions may illustrate what can develop analytically when an open situation is created and maintained from the beginning. The conductor can interfere with the process of group analysis just as he can impede the development of the dyadic analytic situation in terms of the transference neurosis by interceptive interpretations, directions, manipulations, and the inspirational exploitation of transference manifestations. Of course, it is necessary to identify suitable intermediate goals for the group, just as continuous incidental diagnostic evaluation in the course of analytic treatment may result in an effort to set limits to transference-regression—in borderline patients, for example, or in cases where a damaging and irreversible change in the life situation may threaten the patient's future.

We must also take full medical responsibility for our patients in group therapy. For this reason the psychiatric supervision of group therapy conducted by nonmedical therapists is necessary. For example, we encountered an exacerbation of symptoms in the second phase of the analytic process with ulcer patients, and this necessitated bed-rest for some of them. To be sure, these were known somatic reactors, but somatic reactions may occur in the course of group-analytic psychotherapy with other patients, too, just as adverse behavioral reactions—so evaluated first by the nursing staff—are encountered in schizophrenic inpatients undergoing therapy. Such contingencies, which tend to be characteristic of the more effective forms of group therapy, often require medical consultation for their management.

Isidore Ziferstein and Martin Grotjahn (1957) drew attention to the fact that group psychotherapy stimulates acting-out, which may make the therapy more dangerous. The entire group may become involved in the acting-out, so that the therapeutic function of the group is endangered. On the other hand, his fellow members may help the acting-out patient to achieve insight if the situation is well handled by the therapist. When this is the case, the end-result of the acting-out—properly understood, interpreted, and worked-through—is useful for the whole group. Acting-out is a substitute for remembering and is used by patients as a form of resistance. It is, however, also a form of test-acting which, properly understood and interpreted, can lead to recollection and integration. In other words, sexual or hostile acting-out may be enlisted within processes of psychotherapy, preferably as promptly as is possible.

In consideration of how frequently acting-out results from unconscious cues offered by the conductor, and how laden with possibilities for good or evil the group situation is, perhaps the remark about the necessity of adequate consultation will become clearer, if not more palatable. One of the most difficult—and at the same time most important—points in leading a group is the identification of any disturbance in oneself. The conductor is also inside the group, and some of his problems must, of necessity, be resolved inside the group situation. Should he have disturbances which interfere with his function as a conductor and which he is unable to reveal to the group, he is, in principle, not in a fit state for his role. We have already alluded to some common problems (page 22).

It should be noted that the ventilation of experience in the group is not concentrated solely on present or past events, but includes plans, and even fringe thoughts, about the future. Sometimes unaired plans and vague thoughts which suddenly crystallize are acted upon in ways that undermine the group's ongoing analysis. When he detects such resistance it is important for the conductor to confront the group with the inadvisability of making any vital decision (e.g., change of job, residence, or marriage patterns; commitment to marriage, long vacation, etc.) before discussing it with the group—and to point out that some decisions not only affect the life of the group member but the life of the group itself in analysis.

The group dynamics of the therapy group apply to naturally occurring groups of all kinds. The group-analytic situation does not conjure "dynamics" out of thin air; it is, however, a situation designed to make them manifest, a situation in which they may be observed and investigated. Thus its usefulness is not limited to therapeutic benefits; it provides a valuable training experience for sociologists and psychologists, psychiatrists, graduate students of nursing, and students of political science and social work.

In group-analytic psychotherapy the conductor's interpretative task concerns aspects of group functioning. To reach an appropriate level of understanding the conductor helps to create a permissive arena for the members to project their feelings toward one another, toward the conductor, and toward the group as a whole, using word language as much as possible. Group members share in the interpretative task, but the responsibility that underlies it cannot be as equally shared. It is this gestalt of "democratic leadership" that makes group-analytic psychotherapy resemble but not duplicate the situation of individual psychoanalysis.

Leo Stone (1961) has drawn attention to the symbolic gratification of unconscious infantile transference wishes through the making of interpretations. These wishes may arise from several levels; examples are the wish for tolerance of excreta or the desire to be given food. The more developed (sublimated) childhood wish that underlies, as an essential, the analytic situation—the desire for verbal expression of sympathetic understanding—is always gratified by this means. The latter gratification is also inherent in the group-analytic situation, and it pertains to the whole great complex of supportive example and instruction offered by adults to children, beginning at the level of learning the representational-communicative function of language itself.

Whatever its resonances may be for each member in terms of his earlier unresolved separation anxieties and griefs, as the group draws to a close all members share in the impending loss of group support, verbal exchange, and understanding. Heavy defenses may be brought to bear against this anticipated loss. Foulkes (1964) says of the focus of interpretative intervention in general:

> The conductor's selective interpretations concern actions, behavior, defenses, processes, content as voiced, all within the context of the group. An interpretation does not become an individual interpretation because it is directed to any particular individual. What is really decisive is whether the configuration, the gestalt, is recognized in its conception and execution (timing, etc.).

The inner group action, however outwardly disguised, is always concerned some weeks—at least two months—in advance of the final session with the impending dissolution of the group. It is important to have as adequate ventilation as possible of feelings about the termination of a group that has in itself become a living entity, and a symbol for each member of his family and his clan. The limitations of analytic treatment in a group setting are most conspicuous at this point. Group members who display separation anxiety, depressive emotions, and multiform idiosyncratic fantasies because of the momentous impact of the group's dissolution will have much scantier consideration than they would have in individual analysis. However, it is necessary to explore as far as possible the meanings attached to the group's termination by each member; reactivations of anxieties, depressions, and other symptoms require careful observation. The conductor must in due course evaluate the need for further treatment—sometimes individual treatment—for each patient.

In view of all these difficulties that surface in group-analytic therapy one can only marvel at the temerity of those who lead T-groups. Although these groups offer comparatively short contact, they not only bring about a stressfully induced, headlong emotional involvement, but terminate abruptly in what can only be characterized as a dangerous pattern—and one which is painful in direct relationship to the technical success it has achieved.

We may outline schematically the overlapping phases of group-analytic therapy as follows:

Beginning	1. Exploratory contact-seeking 2. Involvement and regression
Middle	3. Identification, abreaction, and discussion of defense struggle 4. Insight development and change
End	5. Termination phenomena

As already noted, the end-phase of group therapy is the weakest link in the chain. The conductor needs to keep in mind the danger of degenerative forms of grouping that could emerge as defenses against separation anxiety and consolidate in the absence of adequate consideration within the group. Such degenerative forms have been well discussed by R. Battegay (1971) of the University Psychiatric Clinic at Basle. A group degenerates in both the social and therapeutic sense, becoming a mere crowd whenever members lack interest and interaction is reduced, as may be the case in the defensive reactions of the end-phase. A denial of the group's importance can then become anti-therapeutic. It is also important to guard against an exaggerated glorification of the group and contempt for those outside. This kind of narcissistic concentration of group members on themselves requires analysis lest the members lose sight of the social realities outside the closed circle of the group itself.

VII The Training Group-analytic Group

GROUPS composed of postgraduate students in sociology, psychology, and nursing differ from the usual groups of psychoneurotic patients in group-analytic therapy in an important respect; members are not complete strangers to one another, being in varying degrees of contact in work and social activity outside the group. They are thus halfway between the situation of those composing a natural family group and those strangers brought together for the sake of analytic group therapy. Their mutual acquaintance is, however, enough to cloud the discernment of patterns of transference distortion, and it presents particular problems in regard to acting-out outside therapeutic sessions. In an effort to overcome these disadvantages in one of these groups we tried to bring into the twice-weekly group therapy sessions as much material as possible that related to current life experience, so that adverse developments in outside interaction could become optimally available for analysis, and be retained within the therapeutic orbit.

In this group-analytic group of postgraduate students a schedule that called for two meetings a week instead of the more usual one meeting permitted the prompt recognition of disruptive emotional currents and transference interpretation of intra-group hostilities. This circumstance not only facilitated group cohesion but acted as a prophylactic against any hostile acting-out that might have occurred in social and work contacts outside the group-therapy situation itself. Acting-out which is detrimental to oneself and others can take insidious forms; it is not confined to dramatic episodes.

Not the least important feature of the group-analytic group is its provision of a laboratory for the study of intra-group hostility. It is self-evident that in this atomic age, with the boundaries of space giving way, man needs to know a great deal more than is currently known about this unhappy aspect of life, about the source and management of the destructive forces within all of us. Group-analytic psychotherapy offers an important road toward understanding some of the most urgent social problems of our time, for it leads into the prehistoric aspects of individual psychology. It is altogether misleading to think of the group-analytic process as being more superficial than individual treatment, or to believe that any psychotherapist is entitled to embark on such a venture without adequate preparation. As Freud wrote (1921):

> We must conclude that the psychology of the group is the oldest human psychology; what we have isolated as individual psychology, by neglecting all traces of the group, has only since come into prominence out of the old group psychology, by a gradual process which may still, perhaps be described as incomplete.

It is sad that inter-group conflicts are even more difficult to deal with than those developing within a group. Actually, of course, the reduction of *esprit de corps* within a group—sometimes within a very large and heterogeneous group—finds an easy and convenient antidote in displacement of negative feelings toward an out-group. In such a case the displacement may be mobilized by a dual deployment of efforts toward integration and propaganda directed toward agitation (Ellul, 1965). Throughout recorded history leaders having difficulty in maintaining their power have awakened fear and hatred against outsiders, and appealed at the same time to highly patriotic sentiment as a means of insuring group solidarity and increasing their own popularity. These formations of group paranoia, often paraded as sacred ideologies, threaten our very existence and the continuation of what we know as civilization. Accordingly, it is fortunate that educational opportunities to become acquainted with the functioning patterns of groups have been welcomed by some universities, social service agencies, and non-profit public groups, as well as by private industry.

Man is a social animal and functions best in small groups. When he lives in the midst of a large aggregate such as a modern city he is usually committed in some degree to several large as well as a number of small reference groups. Living thus becomes increasingly fragmented, complex, and stressful. Training in group dynamics, fostered by the work of Kurt Lewin (1936) and influenced by the theories of W. R. Bion (1961), is designed to answer the felt need to learn more about how to live successfully with groups of other people. Its avowed purpose is educational rather than therapeutic, and its concern is to deepen the understanding of the multiple aspects of leadership and followership in today's society.

The work of groups under present-day conditions is all too often grossly impeded by regression phenomena characterized by anxiety, depression, and rage. Bion exemplified disruptive group behavior in: (1) the fight-or-flight group, in which members destroy or escape from the explicit agenda; (2) the dependency group, in which members helplessly try to follow a leader without assuming responsibility; and (3) the "pairing" groups whose members form cliques with unconscious fantasies of producing a new leader.

The methods presently used in such group-relations training remain far from satisfactory. They involve a high risk of considerable psychic disturbance and yield results that are meager in comparison with the insights provided in group-analytic psychotherapy. L. A. Gottschalk (1966) observed that the failure of leaders to provide a helpful structure for the group process tends to induce transference distortions that are not adequately subject to reality-testing. Moreover, in the general absence of effort to establish a basically supportive milieu, excessive competition within the group may be encouraged. In the Kafkaesque moral environment that is more or less deliberately engendered, psychopathological reactions are common, although few frank psychotic reactions occur. Steven L. Jaffe and Donald J. Scherl (1959) describe two patients with acute psychoses precipitated by T-group experiences, and they note that special problems arise with the termination of such a group, which is often planned to provide intense experience within a few consecutive days. Many participants leave such an experience in a "high" state which is often followed by a mild-to-moderate depressive "low". Jaffe and Scherl believe that participants may not have obtained sufficient perspective on the T-group experience before leaving it. Kuehn and Crinella (1969), recognizing the stressful aspects of sensitivity training so conducted, contend that at least four classifications of persons should be excluded from T-groups: psychotics, characterologic neurotics, hysterics, and individuals in crisis. Were their proposal taken seriously, there would perhaps be few clients for T-groups.

Group-dynamics training has been advocated for residents in psychiatry, and has been used in some residency training programs on an entirely optional basis, with residents participating in groups composed of both nonprofessionals and physicians. One resident in psychiatry has provided his impressions of such a mixed group. In reading them one should note that this was a pre-analytic experience for the young physician. His account leads to the opinion that only an excessively masochistic individual would repeat such an experience without having special motivation to do so! As for leaders or consultants repeatedly involved in such stressful performances, screening for problematic sadistic character deformations, however rationalized, should be considered. It seems to me that screening should be primarily concerned with the leadership, and that appropriate screening would probably alter the character of the proceedings which, in themselves, are inescapably an invitation for any who delight in provocation.

IMPRESSIONS OF A TAVISTOCK GROUP EXPERIENCE

It is remarkably difficult for me to bring together my thoughts about the Tavistock Conference that ended only twelve days ago. I suppose this is because of the nature of this type of conference. I mean particularly the unusual amount of anxiety mobilized in myself—and apparently in others—by the experience. Of course, it's painful to recall anxious emotional experiences. However, these are my impressions.

I purposely went to this conference with very little foreknowledge about it, although I knew that the basic aim was to study inter- and intra-group activity, and that the conference would be rather highly structured although nondirective. I also expected intense interpersonal interactions to occur in the meetings.

The first encounter with the staff was remarkably cold and distant. The conference staff director read a brief statement outlining the basic aims and principles of the conference. There was no time for discussion or questions. I felt even more uneasy and defensive than before after this confrontation. I noticed that others seemed rather angry at being handled in such a heavy-handed way, but I accepted it matter-of-factly enough. I suppose this was the first indication of my view of authority as omnipotent. The rest of the first day was taken up with small-group meetings (each consisting of ten members and addressed to a study of its own interchange) and large-group meetings, in which the aggregate of five small groups studied its own behavior. The small-group meetings, of which there were seven in the entire conference, pleased me most, probably because I was familiar with the small-group setting, both as a member and a conductor. The group leader from the conference staff was emotionally distant from the group members, and made infrequent interpretations, group-oriented and cold, chiefly directing attention to the assigned task. My major concern in the small group was how to handle this "cold fish" of a leader. The degree of independence I might be experiencing at the time dictated my approach to him; I would either ignore him or be defiant toward him, possibly suggesting that the group did not have to pay attention to him. On the other hand, I might follow his interpretations and suggestions submissively and obediently. I felt tremendously frustrated at the absence of any clear indication from him as to how much autonomy I might have as a group member. I think I avoided much uneasiness toward the authority figure by turning my attention toward group members, many times taking the role of a "good group leader"—I suppose to fill the obvious deficit. I also found solace by pairing with several group members, either overtly—with an assertive young woman, or covertly—with an older, warm, and friendly man (in both cases inside and outside the group itself).

As the small group progressed, my attitudes toward various members shifted, and negative and positive feelings were strengthened. I must admit, though, that most of my attitudes toward other small-group members and the conductor were never fully investigated or understood, and certainly many of the feelings were not properly worked-through. For example, I felt quite angry toward a young "hippie-ish" man in the group because of our competition for the assertive young girl. I also felt angry at an intellectual and highly controlled male group member. Although these responses were mentioned in the group there was no time to work on them. I certainly recognized the difficulty I was having with my attitude toward the leader, but this was unfinished business, too.

The large group exercised in four meetings on four different days, with the entire membership seated in three concentric rings with two staff leaders in the inside ring and two at the periphery. This was an uneasy setting for me, as I felt none of the cohesiveness that we had in the small groups. I felt very lonely in an apparently fragmented and directionless crowd. Again the staff directed toward the entire group cold, distant, and sometimes seemingly irrelevant interpretations. The antagonistic attitude of staff made me feel uneasy, but also defiant. As a matter of fact, I began this exercise in the outer circle and gradually moved up into the inner ring as a fringe member of an activist subgroup of the membership basically interested in making order out of chaos. This was the only real effort to confront authority during the large-group exercise. Of course, other leaders were quite outraged at our supposed grab for power and we were severely attacked. I felt very impotent at the group's inability to come to grips with itself, especially when any attempt to do so was thwarted by the group itself. It all seemed hopeless, and a dropout rate of 10 per cent as the exercise progressed demonstrated the hopelessness and confusion that we all felt. I must admit that during several of these large meetings, especially at first, I felt quite anxious and depressed at the lack of direction and the futility of such a large group, in which I was lost.

The experience of the large group appropriately overlapped the inter-group exercise, which allowed the members to divide into task- or interest-oriented groups for six sessions over a three-day period. The appropriateness for me of the overlap of the two exercises lay in the tremendous sense of frustration and impotence I experienced in both situations—especially in the inter-group. The inter-group exercise was task-oriented, without the immediate presence of a staff member, and little was accomplished. Various members of the group, including myself, attempted to exert authority in order to get on with the task we had picked (which was for our group to be the instrument of the entire membership for a rational presentation of grievances, especially anger at the staff, both covert and overt). Our group seemed afraid to follow through with such an onerous task as confronting authority, and spent much time struggling over small and relatively insignificant problems such as the wording of statements, methods of presentation, etc. The leadership problem was finally solved by a general-consensus appointment of the black female member as "moderator". As the exercise progressed the group became more and more diffuse and impotent and finally made a token presentation of a very minor point to the staff group—after other task groups had made major assaults on the staff over major issues. For me the inter-group exercise was the most difficult because of our inability to become a cohesive, aggressive unit with momentum toward the completion of our task. Consequently I became a rather passive member of the group and felt more like an observer than a participant. I was greatly relieved at the finish of this exercise.

The last group exercise in which I took part was the application group which met with a staff member five times toward the end of the conference. Its meetings were small, very informal, and unstructured, with free intellectual discussion between the staff consultant and members. They were a remarkable relief, and helped me integrate the experiences of the small-, large-, and inter-group exercises with the reality of interpersonal and personal group situations. Members gave the consultant practical problems from their jobs, and an effort was made to understand such difficulties as competition, the use and misuse of authority, leadership and followership, etc.

I should like to summarize my impressions of this conference. The meeting was well worth while for me because of the experience of participating in the various exercises with attendant emotional response on my part and on the part of others, and because of the intellectual knowledge gained. I should point out that the four types of exercise discussed took place simultaneously, and attitudes gained in each definitely affected interactions in others. Also, a considerable amount of interpersonal activity took place outside the planned events; this was mainly among members, but also occasionally included staff. It would be hard to describe fully and precisely the complex nature of the interpersonal relationships of conference members outside planned groups. I restricted myself to a fairly large number of relatively superficial interpersonal relationships, and one closer pairing with a woman. There seemed to be pairing throughout the membership, but I doubt that much actual sexual activity took place. Actually, because of the extreme emotional closeness in the groups, I had a slight tendency to retreat during my free time, though I managed active participation in all tea and cocktail hours. I was usually exhausted at the end of the day (11 or 12 p.m.), and went to sleep without difficulty. I usually dreamed about aspects of the conference that had made the most impression on me—usually situations of frustration in groups. Early in the conference I awakened an hour or so early and spent the time ruminating about new and difficult interpersonal problems in the conference. I believe that many members had varying degrees of difficulty in sleeping, and I noted also some overt evidences of anxiety, such as gastro-intestinal complaints and headaches. I'm sure that most members—and especially those who took part actively and honestly—felt quite a bit of anxiety and depression. It may have been evidence of discomfort that we all rushed away after the final meeting. It seems appropriate to relate the comment of another member during the conference. We were in the men's room urinating when he turned to me with a look of despair. "This seems to be the only place in this God damned conference that one knows what he's doing", he said.

VIII The Learning Group

THE earliest figure-ground structuring of visual and other perception is instinctually embedded in the inborn dynamics of brain physiology, as the discussion on page 138 et seq. will make clear. In the later processes of refining perception and adapting to changing conditions of growth and movement, however, the child gradually builds inner organizing schemata for selecting and interpreting stimulus patterns or *gestalten* in accordance with past experiences of pleasure (gratification of instinctual strivings) or pain (frustration). More adaptive responses become possible when stimuli fall into these elaborated configurations and are interpreted accordingly. When mental schemata for dealing with sensory input develop further into preconscious assumptions, visual perception contributes still more usefully to the entire process of perceptual-motor response. The complex, rapidly operating circular dynamism of "set" itself, appearing in an ongoing course of multiple organizational events between the schemata and the perceptual act of seeing, almost but not quite inextricably fuses them. When what is perceived leads repeatedly to action that serves or fails to serve instinctual strivings, the resultant pleasure or pain interacts with available schemata to check—and often to modify—them. Their modification by experience makes visual perception more useful for the organism's prevailing conative trends.*

Direct testing by physical manipulation of the environment is, however, impossible in the case of some schemata, even some that depend almost wholly on visual perception. For example, many

* Compare Gombrich, E. H. (1969), in *Art and illusion: a study in the psychology of pictorial representation*. Especially in Part One, "The limits of likeness", he expounds the rhythm of schema and correction in the processes of visual perception and painting, and the limits set by style, which is compounded of a developed system of schemata.

children under eight years of age believe, as Jean Piaget (1929) noted, that the sun and moon follow them about and move as they move, and it will take more than a simple denial of this assumption to disabuse the child, who will cling to his belief until he is introduced to altogether new considerations. Unconscious complexes contribute to many schemata. Piaget (1932) also noted that almost any six-year-old crossing a bridge on the way home from robbing an apple orchard would consider it retribution if the bridge were to collapse beneath his feet from whatever cause. The extremism of such a view is determined by robbing fantasies, repressed and unconscious, connected unconsciously with the Oedipus complex as well as forbidden fruit. Physicians frequently see sick adults strongly influenced by residues of childish schemata that posited retribution for acts about which they felt guilty. Such patterns often relate to unconscious fantasy from the symbolism of which the act in question, possibly innocuous enough in itself, derives its burden of guilt. The only way to check the assumption of guilt in such cases is to talk about the views consciously held. In a free but properly directed group discussion any rigid notions an individual holds may be compared and contrasted with the views of others in such a manner as to uncover and challenge the underlying schemata or preconscious assumptions. In group-analytic psychotherapy this exchange may be but a prelude to a probe of deeper determining fantasies. In his article "Analysis of ideologies as a psychotherapeutic method, especially in group treatment", Paul Schilder (1936) commented on these possibilities 37 years ago.

In her momentous investigation of the processes of perception and reasoning, M. L. Johnson Abercrombie (1960) points out that group discussion can accomplish for thinking what the testing of real objects does for visual perception. Anyone participating in group discussion may soon become aware that his notion of what has recently taken place often differs from that of his neighbor, and conscious too of a wider diversity of possible approaches to any problem than he had been able previously to imagine. The group may encourage or even drive him to weigh many newly discovered alternative possibilities.

Abercrombie notes that the serious consideration of how an individual's behavior may be changed for the better by letting him talk, rather than by talking to him, was one of Freud's most important contributions. She also contrasts the methods of the psychotherapist and the schoolteacher; the former helps his patient to verbalize and to reorganize the schemata that adversely affect his life and behavior, while the latter makes available to his student schemata that others have found useful. She writes:

> The teacher's main job is to present new information in a suitably organized form and he is not much occupied with investigations as to how the new information he presents comes into relationship with the old schemata. The new schemata that are adopted may or may not modify the primitive schemata relating to the same subject; indeed sometimes the new schemata can be incorporated without modifying the old very much, and so can reinforce them even if they are not the kind that lead to effective action. For instance, the acceptance that smoking is causally related to cancer of the lung is compatible with the belief that smoking is reprehensible self-indulgence which is punished by disease.

The special teaching method she describes has characteristics of both traditional teaching and psychotherapy; it departs from the didactic lecture method in the extent to which it arouses various kinds of emotion. Discussion among the students often heightens personal affinities and antipathies, since attention is directed to the similarities and differences in personal reaction, particularly as they disclose conflicting basic assumptions about human nature. Students gradually come to recognize that learning is often blocked by emotional reaction.

The teacher becomes a listener rather than principal speaker in these free group discussions.

> Long speeches are inappropriate whether made by teacher or students, and fortunately at these close quarters, there is less protection than in the lecture theatre against restive movements or the glazing of eyes. It is the timing of contributions that is most important.... My main task was to make it possible for students to compare and contrast the statements they

made with those that others made. The first thing then was to encourage spontaneity of speech which was done mainly by listening and giving signs of having heard—hard discipline for one used to lecturing. I tried to be socially reassuring and avoided making statements which could seem to reprove any individual, or even to praise, because praise of one implies by contrast criticism of the others. . . . On the whole, I avoided also explicitly correcting mistakes—unless they were very dangerous ones. Usually statements were challenged by other participants so promptly that it was not necessary for me to do anything.

As a zoology teacher Abercrombie had been disappointed in how little the acquisition of scientific knowledge affected the thought patterns of medical students or contributed to the adoption of scientific modes of thinking. She was impressed with a statement in the report of a Committee of the Royal College of Physicians (1944) lamenting the inadequacy of the average medical graduate's powers of observation and ability to interpret facts. After teaching for three years at the University of London she hypothesized that students would learn to make better judgments if they were to become aware of some of the factors that influence judgment formation; they would then be in a position to consider alternative judgments and to choose from among many rather than blindly and automatically accepting the first. She then evolved a group method of teaching and learning that differed from traditional methods in ways already noted, and in the amount of attention paid to the processes of observing and thinking themselves, rather than to their results. Her course of eight discussions of one hour and a half each was attended by groups of 12 students each. The first three discussions dealt with seeing, the fourth with language, the fifth with classification, the sixth with evaluation of evidence, the seventh with causation, and the eighth with a review of the whole course. Subsequent tests showed that the students in her course did significantly better than a control group of students in four respects: in discriminating better between facts and conclusions, in drawing fewer false conclusions, in considering more than one solution to a problem, and in being less adversely influenced by experience with a previous problem when approaching a new one.

Students who had taken the special course were, in short, more objective and more flexible in their tested behavior than those who had not.

Abercrombie's specialized teaching project was influenced by her knowledge of research in visual perception and by her experience with group-analytic psychotherapy as practiced by Foulkes. Her work, among other factors, influenced Volkan and Hawkins (Volkan, 1970, Volkan and Hawkins, 1971a and b; Volkan and Hawkins, 1972) in the evolution of their "fieldwork" method of teaching clinical psychiatry. The task of introducing new psychiatric residents effectively to the complexities of psychiatric practice is a difficult one; the Volkan–Hawkins method combines the principles of free group discussion (as elucidated by Abercrombie) with the use of periodic lecture-discussion seminars conducted by faculty members other than the regular tutor.

The fieldwork method is patient-oriented. From its meeting room the group observes through a one-way screen an interview-therapy room, connected by audio equipment, in which each group member in turn treats an inpatient. Each treatment hour is followed by a discussion among the members, including the resident therapist. The patient, seen in this setting for every session with the therapist, is observed by the group only twice weekly. The tutor, by becoming an "auxiliary therapist", offers himself to the group as a more experienced clinician who from time to time makes a technical suggestion, but only when it seems beyond the capacity of the group to initiate this for consideration. Otherwise the aim is to keep the group functioning in free discussion. To enhance the cognitive value of the course members of the psychiatric faculty are invited to conduct seminars pertaining to the clinical problem with which the group is currently wrestling.

The background of the fieldwork method includes Dr. Volkan's long experience of psychotherapy with schizophrenic patients, both on an individual and group basis. In this work he was especially impressed with the importance of identification with the therapist as a factor in ego building (Volkan, 1968). In his group work with schizophrenics he cultivated an educational as well as emotional involvement, one focused on the teaching of basic ego functions.

At the hospital where he had worked the patients were divided into clubs and each club had an attendant as a group leader. Each morning would start with the grouped patients receiving "reality news", an account of the weather and its probable immediate changes, a statement concerning the time of the month and current events. Each member would then be invited to identify himself and to talk about himself. During the day these schizophrenic patients stayed together, eating and playing as a group, having formal group-therapy sessions also.

It is beyond the present purpose to discuss all that is involved in the learning group that combines direct observation of patient–therapist interaction, seminars with "guest experts", and preceptorship teaching, but two remarkable features, *echo phenomena* and *termination phenomena*, deserve mention. The first illustrates the pervasive importance of unconscious identification in groups, which builds expedient adaptations and defenses and permits the use in learning of those resonations that block learning if they are ignored. The second indicates to what extent an intensive group process of libidinal binding takes place when a long time and many meetings are involved, like the processes of profound identification that may be ignored but not avoided.

A basic difference between a therapy group and the learning group engaged in the Volkan–Hawkins fieldwork is that the specific objects differ, but, more importantly, clarifications and interpretations in the latter are made only in relation to patient-oriented issues. The teaching supervisor interprets psychic processes, including anti-therapeutic counter-transference reactions awakened in the therapist by the patient, and in other group members by witnessing the therapist at work with his patient.

For example (Volkan and Hawkins, 1971b), when a young man suffering from paranoid schizophrenic disorder talked in a bizarre way to the therapist about obvious oedipal struggles with his father, considerable anxiety was generated among the residents. Soon the free group discussions contained many references to the fantasied and feared power of the tutor, and in connection with their anxiety the residents voiced their fear that he would give them an examination about this patient when the sessions were completed.

Challenged to declare his intentions, he made it clear that he had no such plan.

During the following week as guest consultant I talked to the group, as requested, about the Oedipus complex. The next consultant answered their questions about homosexuality, both topics having been raised by the residents during their discussion of the patient's overtly expressed (and denied) problematic relationships with his father and mother, and others. At the end of the month I was asked again to lecture briefly on Freud's discovery of the Oedipus complex, and to discuss it. In response to some obvious aspects of the patient's problems, noted by the group, I briefly recounted the story of Polycrates:

> The conquering tyrant of Samos had been repeatedly fortunate and victorious in battle, expanding his territorial domain. Amasis, King of Egypt and his ally, became uneasy at his continuously successful career and warned Polycrates to part with something he valued excessively, in order to appease the rising anger of the jealous gods. With great ceremony Polycrates thereupon threw into the sea an engraved gem of extraordinary value, a piece of booty from a defeated and illustrious foe. A few days later a fish was presented to the tyrant at his banquet table, and the ring of Polycrates was found inside it. It was evident to all that the gods had refused his sacrifice. Amasis now renounced all friendship with a man so doomed by the gods, and it was not long after this that Polycrates, entrapped by a satrap jealous of his good fortune, was crucified.

After this story was told some of the residents talked about other Greek myths having no obvious connection with the subject being discussed. An atmosphere of intense competition with me became evident. Then one resident familiar with my British background began speculating about the motivation of the British Empire in seeking what he saw as world conquest. No interpretations were made.

Although Dr. Volkan prescribed no medication, feeling that the group needed an understanding of the psychological processes unmodified by drugs, the therapist-resident and others in the group decided during the fourth week to start the patient on tranquilizers without consulting the tutor, in a serious challenge to his authority.

During one session the patient kept throwing questions at the therapist like a parrot. "What is at the bottom of all this?" he asked repeatedly. Following this hour the residents put parrot-like questions to the tutor, asking such things as "What are the descriptive differences between 'loose associations' and 'flight of ideas'?" Although the questions of the patient and the residents merited deeper interpretation the tutor responded at first by replying to them at face value, although later he felt that the situation was ripe for interpretations that would link the residents' motivations in parroting questions with the patient's reasons for doing the same.

The tutor shortly drew their attention to parallels between the patient's struggles with his father and their struggles with him, pointing out that by reflecting the patient's struggle in their sessions they were gaining experiential, first-hand information about it. With this interpretation they talked more freely of their anxieties and rebellious feelings, and finally spoke of their enterprise in administering medication to the patient behind the tutor's back. The tutor then secured another "guest expert" to talk about psychotropic drugs in the treatment of schizophrenia.

Experiential learning is promoted throughout the fieldwork as accompaniment to didactic seminars and discussion of technical suggestions. Some of the patient's psychodynamic constellations always appear within the learning group, as if the shadow of the patient's object-relatedness were falling across it. As group members engage in these here-and-now echo phenomena, and closely identify with the patient whose severe conflicts resonate with their own, episodes of "acting-out" can be used in the service of the learning task.

Another example may further underline the echo phenomena. A young male patient with symptomatic hysterical disorder signed out of the hospital against medical advice after two weeks of treatment. He was motherbound, and it was his mother who influenced his departure despite objections from the father. He left only after considerable family altercation, which he reported to his therapist. A manipulative competition for authority over the boy was evident; he seemed to be torn apart between conflicting pressures as his mother had him released from inpatient care. Since this occurred in the middle of the general learning plan based on his case, it caused fragmentation in the treatment group. The residents turned against the social workers, and tried to pit the tutor against the supervisor of the ward where the boy had received care. The tutor then helped group members to see similarities between their own behavior and that of the members of the patient's family. During discussion of these likenesses some residents made repeated slips of the tongue, referring to people interchangeably in a way that would indicate incest, calling a brother "the husband", the mother "the wife", etc. These parapraxes were called to the attention of the group, which then discussed the report of a resident that the mother and son had behaved like lovers on the ward, with kisses, protestations of love, and fondling. Other evidence of the patient's unconscious incestuous attachment was noted.

The resident therapist, a mother of five, forgot to attend the next didactic session. At the next free group discussion she spoke of overlooking the appointment, and expressed surprise at her identification with the patient's mother, realizing that she had stayed at home to perform in a motherly way a service for her son that he was perfectly able to manage himself, and seeing in some measure her own oversolicitude reflecting the attitude of the woman who had tried to make herself indispensable to her son.

The learning group most nearly resembles a therapeutic group as it approaches termination. At this time, threatened by group dissolution and defending themselves against separation anxiety, some members depreciate the intense learning experience the group has provided. The feelings of the residents about termination need time for ventilation. It is usual for a change of emphasis to take place spontaneously about two months before the scheduled end of the course, with attention moving from the patient-oriented clinical material to the group's own emotional interaction. No special attention was given to this phase of separation with the first group of residents, but experience soon indicated the necessity of paying more attention to group processes at this time in the life of the group than to direct learning of clinical psychology. Clarifications and interpretations about the group's termination, along with the encouragement of the ventilation of thoughts and feelings, have helped residents to appreciate the importance in psychiatric work of concepts of loss and restitution.

Learning groups may aim to modify thought and behavior, as in Abercrombie's attempt to encourage medical students to think in a truly scientific way. They may have homely practical application as in Lewin's (1936) efforts to modify the food habits of housewives in wartime. Through group involvement and discussion these women were led to include in their family menus such available and highly nutritious meats as sweatbreads, beef hearts, and kidneys, which they had previously regarded as offal. Lewin's experiments demonstrate the superiority of group discussion over lectures and individual persuasion in changing attitudes toward food, which are fundamental and notably resistant to change.

Other learning groups are more complex and employ some analytic interpretive efforts. In the Volkan–Hawkins fieldwork program of teaching psychiatry to first-year residents, for example, the unconscious components of the participants' attitudes and behavior are sometimes explored, but only when such exploration will clarify specific aspects of clinical psychiatry currently under study in connection with patient care. More definite efforts to change behavior generally and to engage more completely in analytically oriented psychotherapy appear in some other learning groups.

Learning groups more closely allied to GAP

The attempt of Abrahams and Varon (1953) to modify by a group approach the behavior of certain mothers to their young adult schizophrenic daughters has been mentioned on page 29. Psychotherapy for these women, conducted by a psychiatrist with the assistance of a social worker, demonstrated that interpersonal interactions between mother and daughter aggravated and perpetuated the schizophrenic disorder, and showed that noxious interaction could be alleviated in analytically oriented group psychotherapy.

Rex Speers and Cornelius Lansing (1964) gathered four mothers of psychotic children into a learning group and the therapist (Speers) opened the proceedings with this statement:

> I do not know what has caused your child to be ill, and I'm not sure that we will ever know. I believe that there is an interaction between you and your child, an interaction which began in the child's infancy, which is continuing in the present and preventing your child from maturing properly, and at the same time causing you untold distress. I believe by our meeting together weekly and talking over events that occur between you and the child, and especially the feelings that accompany such events, we can understand this interaction and help you to alter it, to the advantage of both.

This learning group became involved in analytically oriented group psychotherapy. The mothers soon sought to gratify their narcissistic dependency needs through the group therapist. When he refused to be an all-giving mother they turned to their husbands for further gratification, each soon complaining bitterly of her husband's inadequacy. The men agreed to enter therapy chiefly because of pressure exerted by their wives. In the men's group they showed old patterns of emotional isolation that had enabled them to remain aloof from their mothers, wives, and children. Twenty months of therapy, with patient and persistent interpretation, resulted in their entering more actively into therapy, with subsequent improvement in their performance as fathers and husbands. This progress was enhanced as the children became more accessible and human and the wives less demanding because of the improvement effected by their respective group therapies. In general, the vicious circle of events within these families was gradually replaced by a benign one.

Ake Mattsson and David Agle (1973) have more recently described analytic group psychotherapy for the parents of hemophilic children. Pediatricians as well as psychiatrists have for years recognized that children with chronic diseases have many special problems, and have offered a number of methods for maximizing their psychosocial adaptation. We know less, however, about the difficulties the parents of such children face, and the ways in which they adapt to the situation. The study of Mattsson and Agle accordingly deserves special commendation.

Ten parents of young hemophiliacs participated in a series of 25 weekly group meetings conducted by a general psychiatrist (Agle) and a child psychiatrist (Mattsson). Their therapeutic goal was to help these parents understand and master their distressing affect-laden reactions to the serious disorder afflicting their children; these were impeding productive interaction between the sick children and their parents, and the child's adaptation and development as well. This group work was undertaken in knowledge of the fact that brief counseling of the parents all too often did very little to promote the child's independence, his cooperation in his medical regimen, or any reduction of the frequency of bleeding episodes. The special investigative purpose of the meetings was to learn what methods of mental adaptation the parents of chronically ill children employ.

The group process facilitated the ventilation of anxiety, anger, sadness, and guilt—affects which had at times been intense enough to be incapacitating. The parents expressed considerable criticism of medical personnel, and hostility toward them, along with special resentment at their failure to provide helpful counsel. It was a relief for most of the parents to share the experiences and feelings they had in common, and this sharing promoted group cohesiveness. They began gradually to recognize their ways of coping with the chronic stress of having a bleeding son in the family. Their adaptational methods included many well-known psychological defenses, most of them useful in an acute emergency but often inexpedient in sustained family interaction, such as the isolation of dysphoric affects and the denial of a sense of guilt and of feelings of helplessness. Other defenses were consistently noxious to the child's development and without even emergency value. Among these were reaction formation that led to a smothering overprotection, and rationalization that insisted unduly upon the presence of a hemophilic child as being a challenge to the family to achieve a spiritually richer life. Some parents evidenced transient but excessive use of denial, rejecting the reality of the life-threatening aspects of hemophilia in ways that occasionally had pathological consequences for their children. For example, some failed to restrain their children's activity reasonably and exposed them to unnecessary physical danger. Besides using denial and rationalization, all group members had frequently defended against disruptive emotion by heightened intellectuality.

Bibring et al. (1961) have distinguished the mechanism of *control through thinking*, which Mattsson and Agle found conspicuously present in the parents they studied, from *intellectualization*. They emphasize that by the use of *control through thinking* "the control of the frightening situation is not primarily drained of anxieties, but through extended anticipatory familiarization with the danger, an attempt is made to prepare oneself and thus lessen the anxiety". In contrast, *intellectualization* is "a systematic overdoing of thinking, deprived of its affect". Mattsson and Agle point out that reliance on *control through thinking* was a strong motive for the parents in their group, and it appeared to be a useful mechanism in helping them master disruptive anxiety.

It seemed useful, that is, if it did not lead to the parent playing physician to a dangerous degree. Many of the parents confessed to having done so at times, only to regret it later. All parents expressed their gratitude to those physicians who had provided them with repeated dosages of factual information regarding the disease and the treatment procedures. Such information helped the parents to prepare themselves for future changes in their sons' condition.

The group work of Drs. Mattsson and Agle vastly broadened the opportunities for effective learning for these parents as they operated under the ever-present threat of their sons' having another episode of bleeding. A follow-up made after two years showed continued improvement in their self-confident handling of the problems involved in being a parent of a chronically ill child. Each promoted his son's acceptance of the realistically necessary limitations imposed by his disease, and his pursuit of healthful physical and intellectual activities. The group experience stimulated a few of them to serve as "lay counselors" to inexperienced parents of hemophilic children; medical supervision was provided for them as they undertook this useful counseling activity.

The groups we have discussed here have had varying objectives, some being directed to basic changes of personality, others to some facets of interaction, and still others more concerned with cognitive assimilation than emotional realizations. Despite the linking objective of learning in its wider sense, they are a heterogeneous collection of groups. Nonetheless, the factors involved in learning itself, in facilitating learning and blocking learning, are to a very considerable extent unconscious. One who has become sensitized to the unconscious dynamics of small groups through participation in group-analytic psychotherapy is in a better position to be an effective teacher than anyone who has not had this personal experience.

PART II

GROUP PSYCHOLOGY AND PSYCHOPATHOLOGY

IX Psychoanalysis and Group Process: Some Important Unconscious Dynamics

A THEME of fundamental importance to the formation, maintenance, and dissolution of groups appears in Freud's *Group psychology and the analysis of the ego* (1921). This concerns the relationship between directly expressed sexual instincts and those that are inhibited in their aims. The Oedipus complex more or less succumbs to a wave of repression from the beginning of the period of latency onward. Freud writes:

> Such of it as is left over shows itself as a purely affectionate emotional tie, relating to the same people, but no longer to be described as "sexual". Psychoanalysis . . . has no difficulty in showing that the sexual ties of the earliest years of childhood also persist, though repressed and unconscious. It gives us courage to assert that wherever we come across an affectionate feeling it is a successor to a completely "sensual" object-tie with the person in question or rather with that person's prototype (or *imago*). It cannot indeed disclose to us without a special investigation whether in a given case this former complete sexual current still exists under repression or whether it has already been exhausted. To speak still more precisely: it is quite certain that this current is still there as a form and possibility, and can always be cathected and put into activity again by means of regression; the only question is (and it cannot always be answered) what degree of cathexis and operative force it still has at the present moment.

Freud points out that instincts inhibited in their aims always preserve some few of their original sexual aspects; even a friend or admirer desires the physical proximity and the sight of the person who is now loved only in the "Pauline" sense. We may recognize the beginning of the *sublimation* of the sexual instincts in this inhibition of aim, or we may fix the limits of sublimation at some more distant point beyond which there is in addition symbolic transformation of primitive drives. The relevance here is that those sexual instincts that are inhibited in their aims have a certain functional advantage over those that are not inhibited. Freud writes:

> Since they are not capable of really complete satisfaction, they are especially adapted to create permanent ties; while those instincts which are directly sexual incur a loss of energy each time they are satisfied, and must wait to be renewed by a fresh accumulation of sexual libido, so that meanwhile the object may have been changed. The inhibited instincts are capable of any degree of admixture with the uninhibited; they can be transformed back into them, just as they arose out of them. It is well known how easily erotic wishes develop out of emotional relations of a friendly character, based upon appreciation and admiration . . . between a master and a pupil, between a performer and a delighted listener, and especially in the case of women. . . . On the other hand it is also very usual for directly sexual impulsions, short-lived in themselves, to be transformed into a lasting and purely affectionate tie; and the consolidation of a passionate love marriage rests to a large extent upon this process.

When the directly sexual impulsions are alloyed with inhibited instincts they are unfavorable to the formation of groups larger than two. In regard to this proposition, Freud writes:

> Two people coming together for the purpose of sexual satisfaction, insofar as they seek for solitude are making a demonstration against the herd instinct, the group feeling. The more they are in love, the more completely they suffice for each other. Their rejection of the group's influence is expressed in the shape of a sense of shame. Feelings of jealousy of the most extreme violence are summoned up in order to protect the choice of a sexual object from being encroached upon by a group tie. It is only when the affectionate, that is, personal, factor of a love relation gives place entirely to the sensual one, that it is possible for two people to have sexual intercourse in the presence of others or for there to be simultaneous sexual acts

in a group, as occurs at an orgy. But at that point a regression has taken place to an early stage in sexual relations, at which being in love as yet played no part, and all sexual objects were judged to be of equal value. . . .

Freud's investigations of the psychoneuroses yielded the view that symptoms can be traced back both to directly sexual impulsions, repressed but active, and to aim-inhibited impulsions whose inhibition had ceased to operate adequately or had made room for a return to the repressed sexual aim. Aim-inhibited impulsions may have their source in pre-genital as well as oedipal sexual strivings. The failure of adequate aim-inhibited psychic energy often makes the victim of neurosis relatively asocial, and removes him from the usual tendency to group formation. Indeed, a member's neurosis may have the same disintegrating effect on a group as a member's being in love. That is to say, in the ratio of aim-inhibited to directly available sexual energy a deficiency of the former may disrupt any group larger than two as readily as a surplus of the latter. Freud writes:

On the other hand it appears that where a powerful impetus has been given to group formation neuroses may diminish and, at all events temporarily, disappear. Justifiable attempts have also been made to turn this antagonism between neuroses and group formation to therapeutic account.

In his remarks about the degrees of admixture of inhibited and uninhibited libidinal strivings Freud notes the remarkable fact that homosexual love is far more compatible than heterosexual with group ties, even when it takes the shape of uninhibited sexual impulsions; this certainly deserves further discussion. It is also noteworthy that individuals capable of higher degrees of genuine sublimation are less group-dependent and have less tendency to multiple group formations; it seems likely that this characteristic, too, can be partly accounted for by the limited availability of aim-inhibited psychic energy. This has largely undergone symbolic transformation.

The impetus to group formation mentioned by Freud may be provided by pedestrian, inspirational, or even charismatic leadership. Grandiose images of the parents are formed during the periods of infancy and childhood; after the wave of repression at the beginning of latency, the affectionate (aim-inhibited libidinal) ties cathect these grandiose images, laying the basis of the internal ego-ideal on the one hand, and investing the perception of the actual parents with an overestimation of their power and wisdom on the other. As further development brings an increasingly discriminative perception of the self and others, these earlier images recede into the background, although they are still saturated with omnipotence and omniscience. A more realistic appraisal of the parents and others becomes operative, at least in the conscious mind, but everyone still longs to find again—or to be—a god-like personage, unlimited in power and wisdom.* This longing may be reactivated sufficiently to cathect transference-projection of early grandiose images. In this connection Freud writes:

> In many individuals the separation between the ego and the ego ideal is not very far advanced; the two still coincide readily; the ego has often preserved its earlier narcissistic self-complacency. The selection of the leader is very much facilitated by this circumstance. He need often only possess the typical qualities of the individuals concerned in a particularly clearly marked and pure form, and need only give an impression of greater force and of more freedom of libido; and in that case the need for a strong chief will often meet him half-way and invest him with a predominance to which he would otherwise perhaps have had no claim. The other members of the group, whose ego ideal would not, apart from this, have become embodied in his person without some correction, are then carried away with the rest by "suggestion", that is to say, by means of identification.

In other instances the leader goes much more than halfway in initiating group formation, activating the projection upon him of an image of god-like qualities and unlimited power and wisdom. In the more extreme forms of inspirational and charismatic leadership, as will be shown, the leader–follower relationship resembles that of the hypnotist and his subject; something in the bond severely limits freedom of thought and judgment, as though the follower were hypnotized.

* For a recent treatment of this subject see E. Pumpian-Mindlin, 1969.

The cardinal circumstance in the hypnotic process is the way in which the subject's mind is entirely occupied with the hypnotist. The selective and expectant attention so largely concentrated on the hypnotist and his behavior is associated with the reduction of the span of consciousness, and a relative indifference to even massive excitations emanating from any other source. The procedures for inducing the state of hypnosis basically depend on appeals to *awe* and *love*.

The social and professional prestige of the hypnotist, his imposing behavior and self-assurance in issuing commands contribute to the first; a mild and friendly attitude, a low monotonous voice and a restful atmosphere—perhaps a darkened, soundless room—and soothing, light stroking maneuvers contribute significantly to the second. Sandor Ferenczi (1909) showed how the first relates to the child's diffuse conception of the firm, infallible and all-powerful father, and the second or "maternal" aspect recalls the scene in which a mother woos her child to sleep by singing lullabies. The "paternal" or "maternal" induction may not take a pure form; there may be varying and synergistic admixtures of both in an actual induction. Appeals to both awe and love characterize the efforts of inspirational leaders to fascinate their hearers and to secure a following. Old parental adoration and even more primitive beliefs in magic play a part in the formation of groups, as will be shown. The leader may not only incarnate the primal father, but also the glorified, provident mother. In strikingly charismatic leadership the leader may also symbolize the son or daughter who becomes what the follower aspired to be but did not become. In some instances awe is inspired by periodic exhibition of brutality, punctuating more prolonged demonstrations of loving care and of need to be loved.

Much may be condensed in charismatic leadership; the charismatic leader may at different times actually exhibit a succession of characters in a chameleon-like response to mood changes, prevailing conditions, and the needs of other people. But Freud demonstrated that those who have adopted the same image as their ideal model identify with one another and develop tender mutual feelings. The first kind of identification with an ideal model leads to the second—identification with one another, characterized by affectionate feelings (perhaps first engendered with siblings in the course of the early family drama); and aggressive and especially hostile competitive feelings tend to be diverted away from the group so formed.

A few years after Freud's relationship with Fliess had terminated, upon the suggestion of Wilhelm Stekel, who had been in analysis with Freud, Freud agreed to hold weekly meetings with a group of physicians and others interested in psychological problems. Different as these people were in many respects, in their professional backgrounds they were united in their discontent with the lack of usefulness of the academic psychology of that era in its application to medicine, law, psychiatry, education, and other fields dealing directly with human behavior. As Herman Nunberg (1962) notes in his introduction to the Minutes of the Vienna Psychoanalytic Society,

> On the one hand there was a group of men in search of new ideas and of a leader, and on the other hand there was a lonely man who had made important new discoveries and wished to share them with others.

As the Minutes inform us, the members discussed at the Wednesday Evening Group meetings not only the problems of others but also their own emotional difficulties. They often revealed in the group, in an empathic climate, their inner conflicts, their fantasies, reminiscences and problems with parents, wives, children, and even patients. As the Minutes show, Freud often suggested in those early days that analysts require analysis themselves. He realized early in his analytic work that not only can the doctor exert an influence over his patient but that the patient can powerfully influence the doctor. When the patient's conflicts coincide with those of the doctor, the latter may not see them, or may misunderstand them. This phenomenon, which belongs to the sphere of what is now called countertransference, was an early topic of discussion in Freud's Wednesday Evening Group meetings in the first decade of this century. M. Masud R. Khan (1972) suggests that when Freud instituted the Psychological Wednesday Evenings in his own apartment in

1902 he had intuitively grasped the importance of group-analytic experience as an increment to individual analysis. It is certainly clear that these meetings soon had more than an intellectual function.

X Charisma and Political Power

IN Max Weber's* (1954) political sociology power is defined as "the possibility of imposing one's will upon the behavior of others". The ruler's manifested will influences to a socially relevant and high degree the conduct of the ruled when they adopt in their own conduct the content of his command for its very own sake. Weber used the term "charisma" (1947) in the sense of an extraordinary quality believed to give the persons or objects possessing it unique and magical power. The man with his charisma exercises a domination different from that effected by law and tradition; his power of command is *extraordinary*.

Weber saw legal and traditional domination as quasi-permanent structures providing for everyday community life but subject to challenge in changing times, especially times of trouble, when they become ill adapted to the satisfaction of need and may give way to the domination of the charismatic "natural" leader. It is entirely possible for a charismatic leader to support traditional authority and even to oppose necessary adaptational change, but the appearance of charismatic leadership in troubled times often carries revolutionary implications incompatible with traditional authority. The "natural" leader in turbulence is not one in whom authority has been vested, but one whose extraordinary gifts of body and mind cause him to be considered a prophet or hero, a magician or demigod. In the collective excitement of an emergency situation masses of people surrender themselves to his will.

* Weber's thinking became available in the second decade of the century through publications in Germany. The dates given here refer to texts in English.

The charismatic leader dominates largely by virtue of qualities inaccessible to others and incompatible with the rules of thought and action that govern everyday life. The people turn away from established rules and submit to the unprecedented order proclaimed by the new chief. Large numbers of people undergo inner reorganization of their views and self-experience in this process. When, however, the situation demands only that the people adapt to a major change in law that does not require the internalization of relevant ideas and feelings, the movement from the stress-induced inner disorganization to reorganization provided by a charismatic leader is not needed. The relatively bland situation of orderly legal change sometimes proceeds up to a point which then requires the appearance of a charismatic leader to engender a situation in which the allegiance of followers has at least some degree of revolutionary passion. Masses of people are then involved by emotional contagion in the kind of inner psychic process described. Further change in actual conduct is then possible.

Max Weber's concepts, based on his empirical and historical studies, connect group processes with individual psychological events; these have important early unconscious determinants left out of his considerations. His sociological concepts, however, go beyond the clarification and mere description of recurrent patterns in the social process, and invite further reflection and investigation.

In order to understand the phenomena of charismatic leadership and collective surrender it is first necessary to recall the length of the period during which the human infant is completely dependent on his parents for survival and growth. During the first six months of life the entirely dependent infant approximately doubles his birthweight under favorable conditions, and within a year trebles it. Throughout this heavily incorporative early phase of extra-uterine existence, the mother (or mother-substitute) must provide adequate nutrition for the geno-genic program of the changes involved in such growth. The child's need for a foundation of psychic strength is a counterpart to this somatic dependence, and, indeed, reaches far beyond it; the foundation can be achieved only by an evolving relationship of trust with the providing parents during the early years of life.

The charismatic leader fulfills this reawakened infantile longing well. The follower's wish for a self-image altered in the direction of greater strength can be met if the leader appears as an idealized *alter ego* which can then become part of the follower. To foster this idealization the charismatic leader projects an image of himself that is dramatized by selective self-revelation and embellished by invention; significantly, he may have secrets about himself that he fails to disclose. The follower's relationship to the leader may resemble infatuation and enrich the life even as falling in love does, although it does not arouse consciously sexual feelings of love. On the contrary, sexual aims are inhibited as in the parent–child relation. As already discussed, Freud (1921) showed that the bonding process among people who have the same image as an ideal model provides them with feelings of added strength. Aggressive feelings are diverted away from the group so formed, and the design of the charismatic leader may reinforce this process. To pursue further the comparison already made between charismatic leadership and hypnotism, it can be added that the *engourdissement d'esprit* of hypnotic leadership results in a restriction of consciousness, a selective, concentrated, and expectant attention devoted to the hypnotist and his behavior, and a resistance to distractions.

The charismatic leader's charm conveys not only the magic power Weber noted, but also his own delicate need for love and protection. He yearns to be not only a man, but a woman as well. His inner balance is precarious because of the concurrence of active domineering and submissive seductive strivings in relation to his audience. His is the eternal wish of mankind expressed in the mythic idea that once man and woman were one.

It should be noted that recently the prevalent journalistic use of the word "charisma" has given more reference to superficial aspects of amusement, entertainment, and immediately exciting stimulation, often excluding those deeper unconscious connotations relating to an elicitation of a longed-for heroic image, with which the Greek notion was suffused (Weston LaBarre, 1972). This image is often gained more slowly than by methods relying on merely superficial glamour. The unconscious connotations are often quite debased in the way in which the word is now bandied about indiscriminately, especially in connection with Senator McGovern's 1972 presidential campaign.

XI Anomie

STUDIES in group interaction and in individual behavior are mutually enlightening. An examination of social and economic factors as they relate to mental health is provocative and suggestive.

The dictionary* defines *anomie* in the collective life as "a state of society in which normative standards of conduct and belief are weak or lacking". Applied to the individual, it is "a similar condition . . . commonly characterized by disorientation, anxiety, and isolation". Any society in which unprecedentedly rapid change destroys consensus about goals and life-styles, and in which proudly developed institutions and hitherto honored moral principles are more and more vigorously attacked, is almost certain to be uncomfortable for many, and likely to lead some to become "disoriented, anxious, and isolated" to the point of incapacity.

There is a sense of *déjà vu* in present consternation over the state of affairs. It is no new thing to mark the flow of societal change, and to take alarm at its effects. Nearly 140 years ago Jean Etienne Esquirol (1835), a French psychiatrist, investigated the incidence of insanity in France. After a critical and objective evaluation of available data he found no evidence of any real increase in mental disorder during the previous 40 years. A 1953 study of Massachusetts from 1840 to 1940 showed no increase in flagrant psychotic disorder among persons under 50 years of age during that century in that part of the United States (Goldhamer and Marshall, 1953).

Later, however, Benjamin Malzberg (1959) pointed to an increase of 48 per cent between 1922 and 1950 in the rate of first admissions

* Webster's *Seventh New Collegiate Dictionary*.

to all mental hospitals in the United States, and this increase represented a rise from 68·2 to 100·6 per 100,000. Holding the improvement in hospital facilities partly accountable, he asked, "Can we infer from the increase in annual rates of first admissions that there has been a corresponding growth in the incidence of mental disease?" Working with New York State Hospital figures that go back to 1910, he attempted to find a more definite answer to the question. Except for a decrease during the two world wars, there was a steady upward trend in the rate of first admissions, from 60·4 per 100,000 in 1910 to 106·0 in 1950. Correcting for an age-weighting of the population with the remarkable increase of those over 60, he found a genuine rise in the rate of first admissions, and inferred from this a corresponding increase in the incidence of mental disease. We would be ill-advised to be as complacent about the matter of psychotic disorder as the French were 140 years ago.

In any case it is clear that *anxiety* is on the rise in Western civilization. Thomas A. C. Rennie and others (1957) found morbid anxiety in 75·5 per cent of the population of a compact residential area in New York City, and any such statistical study is supported by the obviously increasing use of ataractic drugs. The incidence of *neurosis* and *psychosomatic disease* increases as industrialization and modernization spread and accelerate. *Tension disorders* manifest themselves strikingly in today's urban and suburban existence.

The effect of the social and economic environment on the individual's mental condition is dramatically illustrated in a sociological study that remains relevant in spite of its 1897 publication date. This is Emile Durkheim's *Le suicide*. At the time of its publication Sigmund Freud had only just begun his investigation of the neuroses, and motive analysis in terms of the derivatives of repressed and unconscious strivings was yet to come. Durkheim concerned himself chiefly with the discrete phenomenon of suicide rate within a society, finding that it varied according to the social setting. From his study of religious affiliation, marriage and the family, and political and national communities, he identified his first category of suicide, which he called *egoistic*. This correlated with a relatively poor integration of the individual into his society. Durkheim found that the spread of scientific and other knowledge that accompanied the secularization process under Protestantism loosened the ties binding the individual to his group and contributed to the incidence of suicide. Those still bolstered by the Catholic faith were less likely to take their own lives.

After noting the correlation of suicide with societal disintegration Durkheim proceeded to study the suicide rate in rigidly integrated social groups in which limited individuation is possible, and in which custom and regulation rigorously govern the conduct of life. Such overstructured societies, in which apotheosis is won by those dying for the common cause, have a high rate of what Durkheim calls *altruistic suicide.* Highly formalized and fervent military groups and certain kinds of tribal societies provide examples.

In dealing with *anomic suicide* Durkheim acknowledged the existence of a *collective conscience* which, in normal times, provides supportive "rules of the game" consistent with prevailing and commonly entertained beliefs and sentiments. Studying the impact of the famous crash of the Paris Bourse during the winter of 1882, he observed:

> Its consequences were felt not only in Paris but throughout France. From 1874 to 1886 the average annual increase (in the suicide rate) was only 2 per cent; in 1882, it was 7 per cent. Moreover, it was unequally distributed among the different times of the year, occurring principally during the first three months or at the very time of the crash. Within these three months alone 59 per cent of the total rise occurred. So distinctly is the rise the result of unusual circumstances that it not only is not encountered in 1881 but had disappeared in 1883. . . . The number of bankruptcies is a barometer of adequate sensitivity, reflecting the variations of economic life. When they increase abruptly from year to year, some serious disturbance has certainly occurred.

The reduction of suicide during the two world wars that Malzberg reported is consistent with the usual experience during great national crises. These provide almost everyone with total allegiance to a common cause and unusually active participation in the common life, strengthening the will to live while restricting egoism. In view of this, Durkheim's study of the correlation between economic hardship and suicide takes on special interest. He asked,

"Is life more readily renounced as it becomes more difficult? The explanation is seductively simple; it agrees with the popular idea of suicide. . . ." But he found that the explanation was not so simple, and that the formula connecting poverty with despair and hopelessness could not be extrapolated to guarantee that an individual will place a higher value on life and experience greater joy the richer he becomes.

He found suicides more common when food prices became prohibitive, but the suicide rate did not decline with the coming of more comfortable circumstances. He noted that unusually low wheat prices in Prussia did not affect the suicide rate there, and went on to study the wave of prosperity in Rome initiated by Victor Emmanuel's conquest in 1870. During this period the merchant marine, communications, and transportation flourished with a resultant impact on trade; salaries rose considerably, workers had a higher degree of material comfort than before, the price of bread fell, and private wealth vastly increased. Using precise figures for rates of increase, Durkheim pointed to an unusual rise in the suicide rate, which paralleled the collective renaissance from 1871 to 1877, indicating that good fortune can have much the same effect on suicide rate as economic disasters do. It would appear that *any* alteration in socially cogent regulation of the individual increases his vulnerability to mental disturbance, and that whenever a man's horizon is suddenly extended beyond past limits he may experience anomie as severely as when his horizon is suddenly constricted. Failing to give adequate consideration to the operations of unconscious masochism, Durkheim restricted his explanation as to how sudden wealth can lead to suicide, indicating that the individual with new riches may not be able to cope with the new opportunities it provides. Too sudden a change in either the upper or lower limits of one's desire and scale of living could confound.

He found some of the same factors at work in the breakup of a marriage, identifying *conjugal anomie*, exemplified by divorce. When the partners moved beyond the regulative influence of the marital unit, the suicide rate became comparatively high, particularly among men. Durkheim accounted for this differential by his belief that men profit more than women from the regulative influence of marriage.

The use of the suicide rate as an index to a community's general mental health may take on additional meaning through Karl Menninger's (1963) concept of *partial suicide*. He uses this term to refer to people who are so abusing themselves as to invite premature death. Persons who are "drinking themselves to death" or becoming addicted to drugs come to mind, as well as those who live on the razor's edge by engaging in dangerous activities that can range all the way from drag racing to exhausting work unremittingly and unreasonably pursued. Moreover, there are those who live out a chronologically normal life span at a level far below their potential for enjoyment and accomplishment, thus paying a debt to appease masochistically a deep-seated sense of guilt. Psychoanalytic psychiatry holds that the range of suicide potential, a basic masochism, varies from one individual to another, and that its intensity depends significantly on the experience in infancy and early childhood of family interaction and its impact on the constitutional drives to live or to die. The child's experiences of being fed and weaned and toilet trained contribute to his subsequent outlook; what he loves and hates reflects whether he was accepted or rejected, how he was told about sex, and the part sibling rivalry played in his early life.

The challenges to the traditional concepts of family life posed by contemporary society are ubiquitous and strident. Professor Tsung-Yi Lin of Taiwan (1960) noted in his study of the family that the extended family is being replaced by one organized around democratic companionship, and that the concept of the family as an economic unit is giving way to the economic independence of each family member. Furthermore, such changes vary only in degree and tempo from country to country, sparing no one from the new necessity to adapt. Conservatives blame the adoption of the democratic companionship form of family life for such problems as broken homes and juvenile delinquency, but it is possible that this kind of family structure is an evolutionary adaptation to the changing cultural and socio-economic conditions of modern existence. Dr. Lin noted that family instability, the absence of stable models, conflicts between value systems at home and at school, the impersonality of city life, and the competitive struggle for survival produce anxiety, especially among children. The adoption of new family patterns is almost sure to trigger anxiety among young adults as well, since the parents of those launching forth in new ways belong to another form of society, and are able to offer little guidance to their children as they move into associations that demand new kinds of relationships. The collective conscience about the rights and privileges of parents, as well as their duties and obligations, is in many ways in a state of metamorphosis, and during this process of change an upset in the regulative forces, an *anomie*, creates all kinds of disturbances in the rearing of children—and in the confidence of parents.

Individual psychotherapy of a neurotic patient does not reveal in precise terms the influence of all the social aspects of his life upon the development of his neurosis, however much it may reveal about some of its genetic origins. Our insight into the patient's problem is also hindsight. We are less capable of appreciating the nature of his past experiences and the way in which they came about in his particular family drama than we are of understanding his past and present reactions to them. The retrospective knowledge provided in therapy does not specifically connect all psychic events with social factors that may have set the stage for them. Moreover, we need better records than we have, and a more reliable system of psychiatric nomenclature, before we can draw more precise scientific conclusions about the effects of various environmental phenomena on mental health in general.

Evidence now available nevertheless strongly suggests that the social upheavals in our contemporary society are leading to an increase in mental ill-health. The World Federation for Mental Health has drawn up a plan to conduct comparative studies of different populations with different social developments in order to see how much and in what respects the state of mental health may differ in different societies. We certainly need more investigation of the complex relationship between socio-economic factors and mental illness. As Durkheim wrote in his preface to *Le suicide*, "There is nothing necessarily discouraging in the incompleteness of the results thus far obtained; they should arouse new efforts, not surrender."

In our time one of those who has made new and significant efforts is Bruno Bettelheim (1950, 1960) in his work at the University of Chicago's Sonia Shankman Orthogenic School. From his own inner experience of threatened anomie in Dachau and Buchenwald he derives a living pattern, not for mere ant-like survival, but for new integration and a deepening vision which accepts the challenge of modern mass society. He writes (1960):

In times of great crises, of inner and outer revolutions in all phases of life, situations may occur in which men have only the choice between such a giving up of life and the achieving of a higher integration. Because we have not yet achieved the latter is no proof we are going to choose the former. If I read the signs of our times correctly, we have taken the first steps towards mastering the new conditions of life in an age of atomic power. But let us not fool ourselves either; the struggle will be long and hard, taxing all our mental and moral powers, if we do not want a brave new world but an age of reason and humanity.

XII The Psychopathic Personality and Group Paranoia

DURING rapid social change the diverse multiple identifications adopted by young people in their search for stable identity formation are difficult to integrate. The relatively unstable basic character of the floridly charismatic leader is often peculiarly productive of constructive new inner orientations and outer adaptive life-styles that may become models for youth under the pressure of anomic social conditions, particularly when the young are implacably opposed by those inflexibly devoted to tradition. It is necessary to guard against the ascendancy of a leader whose charisma arises from brutality and a bold deviance from the ordinary, with an outrageous flouting of convention, however acceptable the dependable leader who is incidentally more quietly charismatic may be. The memory of Hitler's outrages is still alive, and the tools of destruction are even more available to a single hand than they were 30 years ago.

Two years before his death Carl Gustav Jung (1959) wrote about the significance of the widespread belief that "unidentified flying objects" from outer space were visiting the earth. His essay showed the world's people in such an anxious state about their imminent destruction and their helpless lack of control over their fate that they long for mastery by superior beings who would rescue them from their own mischievous impulses. A population with highly charged longings and fantasies about a coming savior is likely to look with favor on any bids for leadership that might come from certain kinds of psychopathic personalities. In group-analytic psychotherapy one becomes familiar with *condenser phenomena*, in which the pooling of associated ideas within a group results in the sudden discharge of deep and primitive feelings and fantasies. Such loosening of group resistance, accompanied by an eruption of group anxieties and fantasies, may lead one to suspect the group judgment engaged in problem-solving at this primitive level. Many a paranoid leader has caused others so to resonate to his passion that they develop group paranoia. This response has been massively evident in recent decades, and has, indeed, been recurrent throughout recorded history (Mackay, 1932).

Although society usually rejects the severely disturbed personality (in ways that the psychiatrist often regrets) it sometimes acclaims a severely disturbed individual as an inspired leader and accepts his hallucinations as revelations, or even commands. It is often the case, also, that with the passage of time a leader originally well oriented toward reality may become increasingly narcissistic, brutal, and even paranoid. This process may, as he ages, be aggravated by cerebral arteriosclerosis and other changes that occur in aging tissues. The wisdom of medically evaluating leaders in all societies seems obvious now that it would take little more than pressure on the appropriate button to create a holocaust. This discussion will not, however, be confined to leadership aspirants who are clearly paranoid.

D. K. Henderson (1939) defined a psychopathic state as one in which antisocial or asocial disorders have appeared throughout the life of the individual, or from his early years on. He emphasized that such deviancy frequently arises from severe sickness of the mind. He noted in such conduct disorder a wide variety of aggressive manifestations in which the impulse to hate gathers strength until the affected individual becomes so mentally clouded and dissociated that he acts in "blind fury", with an inhuman disregard of others. Such excited fury, often accompanied by transient hallucination, is frequently followed by amnesia and tranquility (like that following an epileptic attack), but it takes very little to trigger its reappearance. People who display such behavior are typically "difficult to please . . . intolerant of routine, imperious, bad losers, petulant, egotistical, and emotionally immature". Henderson insisted that semi-insane and semi-responsible people can be found in all walks of life, from the highest social and political circles to the ranks of the unemployed, and that they present not only the relatively minor problem of personal nonconformity but the possibility of the commission of crimes of horrendous magnitude.

A marked paranoid tendency may be associated with a high degree of creativity as well as of hostility. The general concept of paranoia is that of a psychosis presenting clearly defined delusions of persecution and grandeur, generally becoming more and more systematized, with no marked tendency to intellectual deterioration. It runs a chronic course; minimal auditory hallucination may occur. In his analysis of the Schreber case (1911), Freud first showed that what was characteristic of paranoia was the use by Schreber of delusions of persecution as a means of warding off a homosexual wish-fantasy. This contribution of Freud's remains important from the psychodynamic point of view, but many analysts now trace the beginnings of paranoid disorder to deprivation in the first year of life.

Leon Eisenberg (1963) warned that the concept of early deprivation should not be over-simplified. Food, protection, stimulation, consistent and predictable interpersonal contacts, and a structured environment are among the necessities for healthy growth, and inadequate provision of any one of these is significant; but, however well-provided the child may be in these particulars, he will experience special deprivation if his mother functions toward him in a pathological way. My own clinical and analytic work with patients having severe character disorder inclines me to believe constitutional cerebral disorder and early deprivation often combine to produce the psychopathic states Henderson described.

Fenichel (1945) wrote that those individuals whose character disorder leads them to a passionate striving for power and prestige are "unconsciously frightened persons trying to overcome and to deny their anxiety". These people tend to find it possible to avoid anxiety by seeking activities that promise to let them intimidate as well as encourage other people. The need to intimidate or encourage stems in such cases from a dual identification with a powerful aggressor and an omnipotent provider, originally the imagos of the father and mother. External power, especially political power as Weber (1947) defined it, is sought to defend against inner dependence and passivity. Heavy defenses are also erected against dysphoric emotion in general, and guilt and anxiety in particular. Political leaders of this character foster scapegoatism to satisfy their own need for revenge; they find or invent an ideology that sanctions the primitive drives of their followers. In their quest for domination over others such leaders fascinate by the simultaneous or alternating display of both male and female qualities, as the hypnotist does. They maintain the cohesiveness of their followers by diverting hostility toward out-groups. What results is remarkably like individual paranoia, but in this case it is *the crowd* that is inoculated with madness.

It is by no means my intention to belittle charisma, which may endow an institution with socially constructive powers, or an individual with the ability to regenerate his followers. That elusive quality of personality that we can call *vitality*, which arises from the intensity of a leader's intrapsychic conflicts and his efforts at reparation, can be as beneficent as it is compelling. In non-political fields—in intellectual accomplishment or in art, for example—the charismatic leader often makes enormous contributions of novel forms of thought and representation, whatever his private life and emotions may be. The ambiguous character of Leonardo da Vinci, for example, with his tremendous capacity for sublimation, broke through rigid forms of representation to original synthesis. Such achievements hint that such geniuses may be biologically important as sports of nature destined to renew and to inspire their fellows.

Anyone who seeks to work with a group, however, to explore the possibilities of collective interaction, and to understand the way polarization divides our society at present, should remember that some charismatic hypomanic leadership inspires only illusory and dangerous attempts at mastery. We cannot yet determine how greatly disease may have influenced history, and we should be cautious about the possibility of following compelling prophets down excitingly devious roads to nowhere. Later, after the prophet has departed, we may restlessly wait around for his second coming.

Seymour Rabinowitz (1970)* points out that Samuel Beckett's play *Waiting for Godot* (1954) reveals tensions which can be observed recurrently in the analytical therapy of groups. The two main characters in Beckett's play, Estragon and Vladimir, both clowns and tragedians in their tergiversations, wait endlessly for the appearance of a certain Mr. Godot, who will, they expect, bring meaning and goals into their feckless lives. They stubbornly refuse to acknowledge his failure to appear. In response to another's cry for help, Vladimir states:

> Let us not waste our time in idle discourse! (Pause. Vehemently.) Let us do something, while we have the chance! It is not every day that we are needed. Not indeed that we personally are needed. Others would meet the case equally well, if not better. To all mankind they were addressed, those cries for help still ringing in our ears! But at this place, at this moment of time, all mankind is us, whether we like it or not. Let us make the most of it, before it is too late! Let us represent worthily for once the foul brood to which a cruel fate consigned us! What do you say? (Estragon says nothing.) It is true that when with folded arms we weigh the pros and cons we are no less a credit to our species. The tiger bounds to the help of his congeners without the least reflexion, or else he slinks away into the depths of the thickets. But that is not the question. And we are blessed in this, that we happen to know the answer. Yes, in this immense confusion one thing alone is clear. We are waiting for Godot to come—
> Estragon: Ah!
> Pozzo: Help!
> Vladimir: Or for night to fall.

The act of waiting for Godot is thus shown to be essentially absurd; the habit of hoping that Godot might appear after all is the illusion that keeps Vladimir and Estragon from facing the human condition.

* In a paper, *Group psychotherapy and the dramatic element*, presented before the annual meeting of the North Carolina Division of the American Psychiatric Association in 1970.

PART III

LIFE, THEATER, AND THERAPY

XIII Sei Personaggi in Cerca d'Autore

IN 1921 Rome was introduced to what George Bernard Shaw called the most original play ever written. The clash of Pirandellians and anti-Pirandellians at the first performance of *Six Characters in Search of an Author* almost caused a riot. The result was symptomatic. It can now be observed in perspective that the play jolted the axis of the entire theatrical sphere; modern drama thereafter was to feel the effects of changes that Luigi Pirandello brought about. In 1921 and the years following, *Six Characters* directed world-wide attention to Pirandello, a man already in his fifties, and transformed the pattern of his personal life.

With these words William F. Irmscher and E. R. Hagemann (1963) began their biographical sketch of Pirandello. In his own preface to this momentous drama Pirandello wrote, "... an artist imbibes very many germs of life and can never say how and why, at a certain moment, one of these vital germs inserts itself into his fantasy, there to become a living creature on a plane of life superior to the changeable existence of every day". We note that he had just written on the previous page that the nimble ministrant of his art, Fantasy, brought "... the most disgruntled tribe in the world, men, women, children, involved in strange adventures which they can find no way out of, thwarted in their plans; cheated in their hopes; with whom, in short, it is often torture to deal". It is thus not immediately apparent that the world his characters occupied was superior to "the changeable existence of every day". It does not seem, at any rate at first glance, that Pirandello had this world under any better control.

Pirandello once characterized his contemporary, Gabriele D'Annunzio, as his opposite. D'Annunzio ignored social and intellectual themes and ethical problems, saturating his plays with sensual hedonism and making each a long hymn to sensation. It is worth noting in connection with hedonistic art of this kind that whereas many perceptions may afford immediate sensual pleasure some also may considerably amplify this pleasure by recalling past gratification. Often they do this by symbolic reference to past experiences and unconscious fantasies rather than by directly recalling the past in the ordinary conscious sense.

It is also possible to arouse highly painful feelings either through a direct recall of things past or through unconscious reference. What is sometimes called "escape art" has its limitations even when it not only gives us sensual pleasure in its form and content but also when it forcibly reminds us of past gratifications in reality or in wish-fantasy. Perceptions leading us to heightened desire and gratification constitute but one aspect of what is satisfying—and ultimately beautiful. The reduction of anxiety and pain is equally important, and in art in which this is the main thrust—as in the art of Pirandello—the artist leads us first into a consideration of gross problems of anxiety and guilt. The work is variously involved in the attempt to master mental pain, for the benefit of both the artist and his audience.

In *Six characters* this attempt seems to fail, and to display its failure. For some it failed altogether that night in Rome in 1921; but it succeeded in good measure for others, including the artist. We perceive creative and destructive forces together in the works of man as in those of nature. It is when we are assured of the domination of the constructive forces, after being kept in suspense for a while, that we feel pleasure and see beauty. It is when we are made to feel the domination of the destructive forces that we recoil at what seems ugly. Our need for beauty is all the more intense because of the gloom and pain engendered by destructive forces within ourselves, and we look to art for evidence of the triumph of life, the triumph of what is good. Sometimes, for example, art provides an experience that externalizes our feelings of loss and somehow offers us restitution and some reassurance. Pirandello's work is a fascinating attempt at this artistic task.

The relevance of Pirandello's life situation to the play is highly significant. In the drama the curtain is already up on a stage occupied by a director who is considering, with his assistants and with actors and actresses, a new production of a Pirandello play called "Mixing it up". Six players edge their way in, declaring that they are characters abandoned by a playwright. At first against the director's protests, then with his reluctant cooperation, and later with his eager interest, they enact a sordid and complicated story about the relations of a man with the wife from whom he has been separated for many years, and with her children by him and by her lover. Everyone in the enactment is obviously tortured and highly emotional, exhibiting love or hatred or jealousy and, above all, shame. The author uses the device of play within play and assigns the man who plays the Father to discuss the nature of reality in life and in art. As Joseph Wood Krutch (1953) observed, without the peculiar setting of play within play and without the philosophical embellishments we should have a lurid and tragic melodrama.

From the paralyzing effect of a sort of Pyrrhic skepticism we are ordinarily saved by what George Santayana (1923) calls "animal faith". Even those afflicted with Berkeleian idealism—unless they are also victims of some form of frank psychosis—act as though the external world exists. Nearly everyone acts for the most part—unless he becomes mentally sick—as though he believed his version of the external world, however restricted it might be, to be a dependable one for all ordinary purposes. Most people act, too, as though they could also make valid judgments about many events in the external world. But as Krutch succinctly states:

> Not merely in one play, but in a whole series of plays, Pirandello carries on an attack against our animal faith and seems determined to persuade us not merely that we cannot make value judgments, not merely that we cannot distinguish appearance from reality, but that the whole concept of reality as opposed to appearance is inadmissible.

When Pirandello shows that his characters behave as most people do—below this philosophical level, without questioning the nature of external reality but as involved human beings—his character of the Father demonstrates the morass of mutual misunderstanding in which they are all bogged down. The Father speaks for the other characters and for his own predicament when he says:

> Each one of us has within him a whole world of things, each man of us his own special world. And how can we even come to an understanding if I put in the words I utter the sense and value of things as I see them; while you who listen to me must inevitably translate them according to the conception of things each one of us has within himself. We think we understand each other, but we never really do.

As our orientation in the world evolves during our infancy, it is quite dependent on the ways in which our bodies function. While Freud was investigating aphasia, Joseph Breuer (Flugel, 1933), with whom he was later to collaborate in the momentous enterprise we all know about, was investigating the semicircular canals of the inner ear. We now know that tonic muscular reflexes operate in concert with reflexes mediated through stimuli from the inner ear, and that all of these and other reflex activities in infancy underlie the orientation in the world that develops further during childhood. Later, the asymmetric laterality of the body and its functions gradually becomes more marked, and by two years of age there is usually a clearly dominant hand. Children's skills develop in a manner which shows the growth of the right-and-left concept, accompanied by increasing awareness of a differential in sensations and skills between the two sides of the body. It is altogether on a body basis that our reliable orientation in space and time is gradually evolved; and this body basis is largely responsible for the "animal faith" described by Santayana.

All this is, moreover, a pre-stage of language. In the early phase of oral development the tongue is already a primal organizer of the self, as Augusta Bonnard (1960) has shown. Even later we can observe residues of this early function. Bonnard notes:

> If we watch young children attempting a troublesome balancing or integrative task, including learning to write, we can often observe the tongue protruded to serve like the offsetting combination of the rudder and the center board of the boat, i.e. as the body's centering point.

Then word language itself, mediated partly by the tongue, enormously and increasingly enhances our orientation in the world. I want only to emphasize here that in *Six characters* Pirandello upsets our equilibrium, our animal faith, and then our confidence in the use of language. We are bound to feel distressed, to experience some vertigo. We can yell in anger as the anti-Pirandellians did that night in 1921 in Rome, or we can reflect and examine some of our assumptions.

But in this peculiar play of his Pirandello was not content to challenge our orientation in the world and the reality testing that depends so much on this organization of space and time. He challenged as well the reliability and consistency of the ego that performs these functions. The inner and outer worlds—those of ego and of external reality—develop psychic representations together, with self-development and ego differentiation from the external world actually being necessary quite early for reality testing to be effective. Moreover, in this one-sided and sketchy account of how orientation comes about I have not only discussed inadequately the development of the body image—that core of the mental ego—but I have neglected the important interactive aspects of mothering and fathering, and of those family and other influences that generally play a large part in the development of the ego during childhood, adolescence, and later.

Suffice it now to note that many critics, Krutch (1953) and Adriano Tilgher (1928) among them, dwell on the dissolution of the ego as it appears in Pirandello's dramas. Krutch writes:

> Moreover and in the process (of the play), the "I" itself, the thing which perceives appearances and becomes the victim of illusions, disintegrates—if, at least, one means by the "I" any continuous, persisting, relatively stable

thing. Every "I" is not merely all the things which at various times it seems to various people to be. It is also all the different things which at different times it has been. There are the "I's" of yesterday, today and tomorrow, as well as what every observer has taken each of them to be. At one point in the play the husband (the Father), who has been caught in a ridiculous and even, in his judgment, a reprehensible act, protests against being judged by it; protests, that is, against the assumption that this action is typical of him or that, as we should say, he is "that kind of man". But from the standpoint of the play this is, of course, absurd. It assumes that he has a character as distinguished from the sum of all the inconsistent things which he does, that he is "being himself" at certain moments and not "being himself" at others. What, Pirandello seems to ask, can a "self" be except what it is doing from moment to moment?

I should have to disagree with Krutch here, and to agree with Hubert Heffner (1957):

That "dissolution of the ego" which Krutch, Adriano Tilgher, and others find the distinctive contribution of Pirandello to modern drama is then, on closer inspection, somewhat like reality to certain Pirandellian characters, something of an illusion. The ego does not disappear in Pirandello's characters; it grows more complex, taking on some of the aspects of change which we find in human personality. In that change, the character is constantly asking who am I—but he is always sure there is an I, different as the I of today is from the previous I's which he has known.

Moreover, Lander MacClintock (1951) sagely observes:

The man or woman (in Pirandello's plays) who flees from unbearable problems into a world of illusion does what Pirandello calls "costruirsi" ("to build oneself up"). He becomes not one but many personalities, which he displays at different times, under differing circumstances.

Thus, in the course of these events, it is not simply the reenactment of earlier ego-orientations but the assumption of altogether unauthentic roles that becomes self-confusing.

There are actually seven characters in *Six characters in search of an author*—the six members of a family and Madame Pace, the brothel-keeper. The paradoxically ludicrous situation of these discarded characters interrupting a rehearsal and demanding to be heard is mixed up with the grotesquely sordid but fragmentary story of their lives which they insist upon telling—revealing through Pirandello's art their terrible suffering and their disturbed relationships. This mingling of the comic and the tragic, the grotesque and the sad, displays Pirandello's vision of life, a vision he had earlier expounded in his treatise *L'umorismo* (1908).

Four of the six family members cannot agree about what has happened. Years earlier, the Mother had departed to live with the man who had been the Father's secretary. It seems that the Father, driven by "The Demon of Experiment", had sent her away. He had observed the loving relationship and mutual sympathy growing between his humble wife and his gentle clerk, and this had made him so uneasy that he dismissed the clerk. Then, when his wife had seemed to pine for the clerk, he sent her away too. After going to live with the secretary she had three illegitimate children—the Stepdaughter, the Boy, and the Child. She had already borne the legitimate Son, who, according to the Father, was brought up in the country away from his mother so that he could be strong. The Father insists that he sent the Mother away out of compassion, but the Mother believes that he tired of her and drove her away. The Stepdaughter, however, maintains that the Mother did abandon the Father and the Son, and that her denial is being made in an effort to win back the affections of the estranged Son. The Father and Stepdaughter also have differing views about his surreptitious interest in her when she was a schoolgirl. Although the Father insists upon his continuous interest in her welfare, she takes a cynical view of his reasons for watching her going home from school.

The play within the play pivots on the beginning of a sexual involvement of the Stepdaughter with the Father in a bordello before he is made to recognize who she is. The girl uses the incident in support of her contention that the Father is a lecher; she seems bent on vengeance throughout. The Father insists that his whole being cannot be judged by the one aspect of his character revealed in his conduct in the bordello. The Son does not want to know about any part of this event, and the Mother, overcome with shame, spends much of her time weeping. The two younger children suffer in silence until one is drowned and the other shoots himself. There is much altercation between the director, the actors, and the characters, in which Pirandello demonstrates the formidable problem of Zola's *tranche de vie* as a theatrical possibility.

Further, Pirandello shows that the allegedly realistic theater distorts life. The director wants to pack all the characters into a neat little framework and then act what is actable. He wants action, and dislikes long speeches, so he wants to cut the Father's. According to Alvin B. Kernan (1958):

> The Father is trying desperately to convey his agonized recognition of guilt but at the same time to present his view that sins of the flesh are natural to man and that one unfortunate slip cannot alone characterize a man. . . . The Stepdaughter finds the author-manager equally intractable, for she feels that she is the innately modest but unfortunate victim of circumstances while the Father is no more than a lecherous brute. To realize this she insists that the Father in the seduction scene speak the line he actually used in the bordello, "Ah, well, then, let's take off this little frock". And she wants herself presented as a noble heroine who is forced to do so. The author-manager refuses to handle the scene in this way, and the Stepdaughter points out to him that all he wants to do is "to piece together a little romantic sentimental scene out of my disgust, out of all the reasons, each more cruel and viler than the other, why I am what I am". The author-manager points out realistically that since the Father was not her first customer, she is not entitled to the modesty which she feels she has. The suffering of the Mother, the Son, and the two young children eludes the author-manager altogether, for how can he do anything with a young man who refuses to talk or act, a mother who cannot speak more than a few lines without breaking into sobs, or young children who wander aimlessly and silently about the stage throughout the play?

I have lightly limned some of the features of the *dramatis personae* and of the plot, the characters, and the action, and I have especially drawn attention to the fact that in this extraordinary play the dramatist's problems are discussed side by side with those of ordinary mortals. The dramatist in this case was, of course, really Luigi Pirandello, and, as he recounts in his preface, he has not adequately presented the drama in which the six characters are involved; he has presented them as characters in another play which "they don't know and don't suspect the existence of". It is the externalized drama of a rejected inner drama. Had the characters been accepted by his imagination their drama would have been organized altogether differently.

In his preface Pirandello discusses the allegorical symbolism of some dramatic productions that start from a concept—perhaps a moral truth—and provide the demonstration of the concept. He pointed also to that other drama which exhibits "figures, affairs, landscapes which have been soaked, so to speak, in a particular sense of life and acquire from it a universal value". Thus, according to Pirandello, the dramatist can accept in his imagination only those characters whose action will give his production meaning and value. These six characters, with their particular family drama, kept reporting their sad stories in turn, each shouting his own reasons into Pirandello's ear in the solitude of his study. First one would appear and project his "disordered passions" and then another would do the same, much as they do in the play to the unhappy manager. Pirandello, at any rate, describes their haunting presence as bordering on hallucination (as in eidetic imagery). He says:

> Now, however much I sought, I did not succeed in uncovering this meaning (a meaning of universal value) in the six characters. And I concluded therefore that it was no use making them live....

However, as creatures of his spirit they would not be denied, and so he writes:

> Thus it is that while I persisted in desiring to drive them out of my spirit, they, as if detached from every narrative support, characters from a novel miraculously emerging from the pages of the book that contained them, went on living on their own, choosing certain moments of the day to reappear before me in the solitude of my study....

It was in 1918, three years before the production of *Six characters* in Rome, that Pirandello's wife Antoinetta was finally committed to a sanatorium. For about 18 years he had been increasingly exposed to her depressive and paranoid outbreaks, which sometimes made life unbearable for him and for his children. For 15 of these years, despite the advice of his friends, he had refused to have her sent away, and endured her hysterical attacks and her jealous paranoid accusations. He withdrew from social life in an effort to quell her suspicions of his infidelity, and in response to her bullying turned over to her the control of the family finances. During the war years his sons were sent to the front, his wife grew more violent, and his daughter Lietta attempted suicide to escape her mother's persecution. The war ended with a reunion with his children and a new beginning for Pirandello. According to Irmscher and Hagemann (1963):

> Throughout his years of seclusion, and particularly during the dark years of the war, Pirandello wrote relentlessly and passionately. By 1918 he had published six collections of poems, six novels and hundreds of short stories, and had turned serious attention to the drama, a form he confessed he hated before the war. By 1921 his royalties permitted him to give up his professorship and to devote full time to writing and directing his own plays. The production of *Six Characters* in Rome, New York, London, Paris and Berlin between 1921 and 1924 brought him international fame.

We are trying to penetrate into the relationship of Pirandello's life to his play *Six characters* not for its own sake, but because of the illustration of certain psychic processes it provides. When the Mother protests in the play that she had been driven away, and the Father talks of his compassion, it would appear that some otherwise inadmissible wishes were given disguised expression, however much they remained in conflict with other ideas and other ideals. Although the Father is a man about the same age as Pirandello was when he finally committed his wife to an institution, he is curiously like descriptions of Pirandello's own father, with his alternation from suave to violent manners; and there were many aspects of Pirandello's behavior strikingly like those of the sensitive and long-suffering Mother who was so devoted to her home. In the play, then, there are elements of the author's primary family drama and of his childhood; there are, as we would say, dramatized introjects, and the incest theme, with its indications of problems between father and daughter, and between mother and son, is more or less outspokenly revealed. The bitterness about a disrupted home, as exhibited by the Son and Stepdaughter, is also reflected in Pirandello's bitterness about all the usual binding conventions. For he became an ardent admirer of Mussolini, who, like Pirandello's Sicilian father, was much given to violent talk and action, unconstrained by the fetters binding ordinary mortals and heedless of the presiding images of the ordinary man.

According to Domenico Vittorini (1935), Pirandello

> . . . looked at the painful circumstances of his life, at his acts and feelings, as if they were the life and acts of another being. He saw himself just as if he were a character in a strange drama, the creation of a cruel and fantastic artist. This harrowing contemplation induced the madness that he gives to his characters. His was a terrifying madness, and he felt it beating in his own veins, tormenting his brain, searing his soul, withering his body. Yet he continued to live and to work, finding in his art a solace for the tragedy that life had assigned to him.

This capacity for detachment, however marred by a mocking quality, led to Pirandello's ability to plumb some of the depths of conflict and to understand the multiplicity of the ego. His nihilism, however, caused him to overlook in this play the ego's integrative functions and possibilities, although he did expose some of its foundations. His detached and sardonic awareness of human suffering permitted him to have in his imagination a kind of superman control over events that otherwise threatened to overwhelm him; this sense of power allowed him to substitute himself for the cruel God of his own drama.

In *Six characters* he envisioned the group reenactment before the author-manager up to the point where his imagination boggled at having to deal indirectly with his own sadomasochistic problems, and his feelings about the wife to whom he was masochistically bound but whom he finally cast away. He was also deeply involved in his attempts to find his identity as a man rather than as the impudent youth expelled as a student for insubordination from the University of Rome. He needed to find some sort of reconciliation with his father, some resolution of his ambivalence toward him, and some alternative to his sadistically charged image of him. His incapacity to resolve the demands of this essential inner integrative psychological task led to an impasse with his dramatic characters and then the peculiar solution provided by the form of the play. As he explains in his *Preface*, "The poet, unknown to them, as if looking on at a distance during the whole period of the experiment, was at the same time busy creating—with it and of it—his own play." He used his art, which made available a magical supremacy, to defend against his helplessness, and held the products of his art to be more real than reality, abiding beyond the existential changes that end in decay.

The group reenactment of a family drama, the free-floating discussion of life events, the emotional release, and the attempts to understand not only what happened but the meaning of what happened—these suggest the possibility of another kind of situation and of another kind of director-author-manager who as a conductor and healer might monitor such proceedings in the direction of therapy, of resolution and integration. These possibilities presented themselves to Foulkes' prepared mind.

XIV Verbal Communication and Acting

WE have been able to follow in some detail the ways in which a playwright attempts to work through his personal psychic problems on the stage, and this study brings us back to the conduct of analytic group therapy. We have already mentioned (page 7) Foulkes's debt to Pirandello and Gorky as he moved toward his commitment to group analysis.

It was Foulkes (1964) who wrote of the technique of group-analytic psychotherapy:

> ... In the group situation both members and therapist are more active, more concerned with the *here and now*, with the presenting situation, with interaction, relationships, than would be the case in the individual situation on the couch. One might even say that this group situation has socio-dramatic and psycho-dramatic qualities and has certain affinities to the technique elaborated by Moreno.

However, he indicates that group-analytic psychotherapy stops short of psychodrama. From the viewpoint of Joseph Meiers's (1945) polaric categories, it lies between the dramic and the didactic group therapies; while maintaining it as group-centered rather than leader-centered, the conductor steers the situation away from didacticism. It is never entirely one thing or the other; thus although it is emotionally interactional it is also a form of dialectics in the sense of being an investigation of truth through discussion.

The situation engendered in group-analytic psychotherapy and monitored by the conductor is in many ways one of wavering balance. It resembles the drama in respect to a common verbal expression of emotion in which the contours of intonation play a critical part. It differs from the psychoanalytic situation with its couch, inasmuch as the persons of the drama—patients as well as the therapist—are in visual contact, so that kinesics, especially as involved in facial movement, contributes powerfully to the interaction. There is less ego regression than that periodically displayed in individual analysis by means of free association and relaxation. On the other hand, there are more stringent limitations to action in a group-analytic group than in most forms of playacting. The visual contact, the conductor's insistence on the "dialectics", and the presence of those within the group with whom the conductor has implicitly established the ethos of restricted action are important features. Communication, unlike that in the drama and in some forms of group therapy, is restricted to that interaction which involves phono- and photo-receptors and their appropriately stimulating effectors, *the somesthetic receptors remaining for the most part out of bounds.* Thus, as in psychoanalysis, physical distance between those involved is preserved, and the main limitation on action concerns any sort of direct or indirect cutaneous contact. There is no laying on of hands, no prodding with a stick.

Yet, actually, in most group situations, including those designed for therapeutic purposes, there is a marked tendency to regression away from the vocal-auditory and higher symbolic organization of the ego. Such regression, when encouraged, may commence with talk in which visual imagery is vivid, and readily progress to shouting followed by music and dancing and, finally, to other forms of action. It is in such contexts that glossolalia (Abse, 1966), ecstatic crises of verbigeration, makes its infrequent appearance in extreme instances; this is an interesting hysteriform anomaly, and a highly informative one. It is more usual for the regression occurring in a group situation to go no further afield than emotional vocal communication enhanced by touch and mutual pressure, long after the initial, bland, agreeable, and apparently pointless opening exchange of the "language of social cohesion" (Hertzler, 1965). In other cases the regressive phase of "phatic" vocal communication is accompanied by hostile talk and action against outsiders. In short, in many varieties of regressive behavior in groups there is obvious evidence of a descent from semantic speech to "phatic" cries (Weston LaBarre, 1964), particularly in groups larger than those designed for group analysis.

The general structure of the group-analytic group is goal-specific. It is designed for insight therapy as well as for emotional release, with the release to be subordinated to the insight gains. Enrollment is limited in order to allow time for discursive communication among the members. Space and time limitations are set, and sessions regularly scheduled. Pairing behavior is restricted. Such a framework of rules permits the conductor to cultivate an atmosphere in which any regressive episode of a group member is interrupted if it is unduly sustained—goes beyond the time of its usefulness for progressively working-through and affording insight. In brief, verbal feedback from group members and the conductor himself is encouraged for the sake of insight; and this occurs in a climate encouraging to both verbal emotional release and self-revelation for all group members other than the conductor, and one in which resistances against this process are interpreted. The gains in insight generally advance in many different ways those salutary changes, including greater adaptive flexibility, which are the goals of group-analytic psychotherapy.

At this point it might be interesting to consider the possible benefits group psychotherapy might provide for the mentally retarded, who can be expected to begin their work below the "vocal-auditory and higher symbolic organization of the ego" from which the group situation normally begins its ultimately beneficial regression, and whose capacity for insight is poor or absent. In a thesis completed in the University of Virginia's Department of Psychiatry in 1972 Andrew Chmiel notes that Carl Rogers (1942) held that capacity for insight and complete self-dependence, as well as the ability to verbalize conflicts, is required if one is to benefit from psychotherapy. Glassman's (1943) study, however, demonstrated an appreciable gain in I.Q. rating for cooperative dull normal children who were given psychiatric treatment. This finding countered the view that mental defectives are poor subjects for psychotherapy because of: (1) deficiencies in communication skills; (2) difficulties in abstract thinking due to verbal inadequacy; (3) the absence of introspection, insight, fantasies and anxieties, and the inability to examine motivation; and (4) the inability to control or to delay emotional expression, or to seek socially appropriate substitute activities in the face of frustration.

Supporters of psychotherapy for the retardate base their claims on the use of a wide range of techniques, including play therapy, support, reassurance, and directive, non-directive, eclectic, and reeducational therapy, arguing that goals should meet the individual's needs, that reorganization of experience often occurs without verbalized insight, that the security of a warm and positive relationship with the therapist can be highly beneficial, and that verbal and intellectual skills have in this connection been overrated at the expense of recognizing the important part played by feelings and emotions.

Cotzin (1948) worked in a structured group setting with nine mentally defective boys who had made difficulties in the classroom and who had been referred again and again to the Department of Psychological Services. At the outset of the ten therapeutic sessions that took place over a three-week period the therapist functioned in a passive, non-directive manner. The group became "almost unmanageable", with considerable hostility and acting-out. The therapist then assumed a more active role and developed a more structured program. Boxing matches were organized, with pairing according to mutual hostility. To stimulate collective activity the boys were next given an opportunity to do something interesting to them for the benefit of other group members, like telling a story, acting out a role, etc. During the last six sessions the adolescents took part in a game of courtroom, with the therapist acting as judge. Each boy took his turn as prosecutor and defendant, and the prosecutor told all he knew about the defendant. Other boys acted as jurors. The initially derogatory remarks of the prosecutor changed to more relevant constructive criticism as more boys became familiar with the role of defendant at first hand.

Cotzin felt that his program offered defectives something that discussion groups provide for normal people—the opportunity to gain insight from seeing the behavior of others. He also thought the group offered advantages in not requiring the boys to formulate their problems verbally, and in permitting them to obtain insight from the comments of the prosecutor and other members of the court about them. By 1969 P. H. Mann had extended the structured group, beginning each session by asking a question or making a statement. The group then developed the opening theme of: Who am I?, How can I deal with authority figures?, or Why have special education? Mann then used films dealing with social interaction or problem situations involving adolescents, and sessions closed on a positive note with an effort to recapitulate the main theme. Mann emphasized continuous support of group members; he believes in putting a hand on a participant's shoulder and expressing encouragement again and again, and stresses the leadership of the therapist throughout.

Fisher and Wolfson (1953), who used activity-interview therapy, provide a comprehensive description of the stages of group process noted during the treatment of the mentally deficient. They identify six: (1) the testing of limits and the development of transference toward the leader, with abreaction regarding frustrations, the ventilation of hostility and resentment (toward family, school, teacher), and competition for the leader's attention; (2) regression, dependency on the leader for help in previously well-managed habitual tasks like tying shoes, buttoning a coat, etc.; (3) transition from ego-centeredness to group-centeredness, with control resident in the group, especially when the actions of one member affect the privileges of all; and (4) positive sibling transference. In stage 3 there is criticism of the leader whenever his attitude toward a member seems unfair, but members become less critical and more constructive in relating to each other. Group participation is enhanced in stage 4, mutual concern is heightened, and adolescents feel freer to discuss "taboo" topics such as pregnancy, menstruation, marriage, and sexual practices. Stages 5 and 6 are extensions of one another, characterized by a growing interest in "out groups", more probing into and acceptance of community mores. Questions about the lives and habits of normal children and customary ways of doing things outside are asked. The final stage moves into more abstract concepts, considerations about God, religion, the feelings of those outside the group, and matters far removed from the personal world of the members.

It is clear that a *modified* analytic technique is worth considering for populations of patients with limited intellectual endowment, especially in the institution where a small staff is faced with a large caseload. It certainly facilitates the working-through of separation from family and home, and provides a favorable opportunity for positive identification with institutional personnel.

It now seems likely that Trigant Burrow's early efforts in group therapy for patients of normal intelligence foundered on difficulties in gaining momentum for the beneficial cycle of group process described on page 107 which includes verbally expressed insight that results in ultimate improvement. His research focus on physiological measurement accounts for his pessimism about small-group therapy, since such an over-emphasis on the part of the therapist impeded adequate psychotherapy. In the thirties Burrow began to center his interest upon the internal physiological changes accompanying external behavior in groups, and in connection with this focus he undertook instrumental studies of respiration, brain-wave patterns, and eye movements. He was concerned with the physiologic basis of conflict among men, his conjecture being that their inner tensions were an expression of a phylic aberration of the human species. According to him, because of this biological basis for his neurosis the individual is uneasy much of the time with his own kind—sometimes desperately so—and, when confronted by others, is usually defensively concerned with his own identity. Burrow wrote (1953):

> . . . The communication requiring adjustment lies at a deeper level than the customary affect-reactions involved in mental and verbal forms of interchange. It lies deeper than the mere exchange of ideas and affects through the symbol of language. It is this deeper level for communication and contact that phylobiology specifically envisages. For this level embodies the articulation and continuity basically uniting the organisms of the species as those organisms are merged in their common interaction with the environment.*

* In this way Burrow anticipated elements of Foulkes's concept of *the group matrix*.

Actually, his attempts to short-circuit the analytic process were disastrous as far as the promotion of basic personality change in the members of the small group was concerned. His distrust of semantic speech and his belief that salvation lay in more direct contact among grouped individuals arose from his developing "psychoneurological" ideas about civilized man's having become lost in the world of the "cortico-symbolic" and being thus cut off from his "thalamo-splanchnic system" (1958). In this respect he is the pioneer of modern encounter groups and some forms of "sensitivity training", whereas Foulkes developed group-analytic psychotherapy.

It is possible, however, that a group-analytic group in psychotherapy may yet provide the vehicle sought by Burrow for physiological measurement of significant affective experiences. In the psychophysiological study of affects it was formerly extremely difficult for an observer to be present and in a position to make reliable observations at a time when a human being is experiencing significant affective change. Nowadays observers behind a one-way mirror have an unusual opportunity to see the group-analytic group in action without disturbing the essential group process. David R. Hawkins and others (1966), who measured pulse rate, blood pressure, and urine excretion, used a one-way mirror behind which observable behavior was rated independently of the therapist. Their preliminary investigation suggests that group-analytic therapy offers the possibility of long-term study of individuals operating in an observable social situation with an intensely charged emotional component.

XV The Lower Depths

IN 1902, at the peak of Maxim Gorky's literary fame, his play *At the bottom* (better known in English as *The lower depths*) was produced by the Moscow Art Theater and enjoyed a resounding public success. The power of characterization in this play, which is based on Gorky's experience among the poor and wretched, illuminates—sometimes in an ambiguous light—the social criticism and moral message he felt compelled to convey. Alexander Bakshy (1945) stated that Gorky ". . . to a remarkable degree . . . achieved a quality of music in his second play, *The Lower Depths*, but it is music which springs from the interplay of brilliantly expressed ideas and striking characterisation, and not, as with Chekhov, from the lyrical emotion which envelops the action". Like Pirandello's *Six characters* it not only displays the emotional interaction and suffering of its characters, but it presents as well a "drama of ideas" in which the ideologies expressed—the different visions of the world—help to reveal the intricacies of character as well as to forward the action. There is also the specific situation indicated by Foulkes (1964): "Here was a play without a hero, a leaderless group on the stage, driven by strong anonymous forces". This is a play which could not fail to interest a psychiatrist concerned with social forces.

As a young man Gorky had taken a Grand Tour of Russia before embarking on his literary career. He tramped from his native Nizhni Novgorod on the Upper Volga, all the way down to the Southern Caucasus and back again, spending more than two years in this vagabondage. During this time he shared the company of a great diversity of people, among them the lowest derelicts of Russian society. He then became a reporter on provincial newspapers and was occasionally imprisoned because of his association with revolutionaries and his outspoken rebelliousness. Bakshy notes:

> His rebellion was directed as much against the conditions which condemned large sections of the population to a life of squalor and human degradation as against the intelligentsia, which had lost its larger vision of life, its sense of the heroic, and was content to busy itself in the prosaic tasks of personal well-being and professional work. In story after story (*and here I may add in "The lower depths"*) Gorki pictured the world of social derelicts and outcasts whose very existence was a reproof to the existing social order, but who, surprisingly enough, were portrayed as superior beings, rising above their melancholy condition to give free play to their passions, to pour contempt on the weak and the squeamish, and to glory in their personal power and their freedom from conventional restraints.

In brief, Gorky not only voiced social criticism but gave close attention to attempts at defense and adaptation, to ways in which survival is assured, pleasure wrested from life experience, and pain avoided.

In the play, the pilgrim Luka, who joins the Bosyáks ("the bare-footed") in the first act, is important in connection with these defenses. Luka, the soft-spoken dispenser of comfort who is always tactful, who sometimes lies, sometimes advises, and sometimes reveals basic truths about human nature, gradually emerges as their guide. In the fourth act it is announced that he has disappeared "during all that mix-up"—a murderous mêlée in which the landlord of the lodging house was killed—"like unto smoke fleeing from the face of fire". In the last act of the play Luka is discussed by the other characters, and described as a good old man, as compassionate and helpful as "yeast leavening our crowd". But then dissent arises. One man says, "He beckoned them to go somewhere but he didn't show them the road", and another complains, "The old man is a faker". Some discuss with contempt his ambiguous attitude toward truth, and others praise his power of understanding. One passage in this context is pertinent:

> Satin (a middle-aged jailbird given to reading and to the excessive drinking of vodka): Shut up, you brutes, numskulls! That's enough about the old

man! (In a calmer tone) You're the worst of all, Baron. You understand nothing—and lie. The old man is not a faker. What's truth? Man—That's the truth! He understood this—you don't. You're dull, like a brick. I understand the old man—I do. Certainly he lied—but it was out of pity for you, the devil take you! There are lots of people who lie out of pity for others—I know it—I've read about it. They lie beautifully, excitingly, with a kind of inspiration. There are lies that soothe, that reconcile one to his lot. There are lies that justify the load that crushed a worker's arm—and hold a man to blame for dying of starvation—I know lies! People weak in spirit and those who live on the sweat of others—these need lies—the weak find support in them, the exploiters use them as a screen. But a man who is his own master, who is independent and doesn't batten on others—he can get along without lies. Lies are the religion of slaves and bosses. Truth is the God of the free man.

In group-analytic psychotherapy the conductor becomes the one who resolutely respects the need for truth at all times, yet is tactful like Luka. Unlike Luka, he does not purvey soothing lies nor give advice. Is it not possible that Foulkes joined in the discussion about the absent Luka in a certain Pirandellian sense? Certainly he arrived at a position which maintained the analytic attitude in the therapy group situation, eschewed any enactment of the role of heroic inspirational leader in response to the group members' wishes, and remained benevolently at hand "in the face of fire". That he became an inspirational guide within his profession by this example and by his writings is yet another Pirandellian paradox.

XVI Verbal Communication and Therapeutic Regression

IT seems evident that group psychotherapy has an important root in the contrived dramatic productions of the theater, and that Moreno's (1923) notion of giving the stage to his patients and then stimulating their spontaneity arose from a contemplation of the meaning of drama. Another link between the legitimate professional stage and impromptu psychotherapeutic theater can be seen in the older practice in which psychiatrists in mental hospitals encouraged their patients to participate as actors in dramatic productions.

The modern psychodramatic techniques developed in this country by Moreno had precursors to which, curiously enough, the Marquis de Sade contributed, in collaboration with Roger-Collard (Havelock Ellis, 1936). De Sade, best known for his novels concerning elaborate sexual aberration—and eponymously responsible for the term *sadism*—spent many years in prison from the age of 23 on for alleged excesses, although he belonged to a noble and distinguished Provençal family. An ardent admirer of Marat, he entered public life during the French Revolution, after the conclusion of which he wrote a pamphlet attacking Napoleon. The object of his attack saw to it that he was once more incarcerated, this time in the asylum at Charenton as an alleged lunatic, although Roger-Collard, the eminent alienist then connected with Charenton, declared him sane. He spent 13 years of his old age so confined, and during his sojourn in the asylum he wrote and produced plays for his fellow inmates to enact (Weiss, 1966). In the early nineteenth century, as an old man, he was insisting on his right to conduct dramatic experiments with human beings.

Group-analytic psychotherapy is more permissive than most forms of playacting in which a prepared script is adhered to; participants are encouraged by the preparation of the situation to be spontaneous within the limits established. It is related to the drama of ideas, in which the exchange of ideas is the *raison d'être*, and ideas are given free verbal expression, and it is also related to that serious drama which explores character and conflict, ethical dilemmas, and human passions by whatever mode—naturalism, realism, symbolism, expressionism, etc.—or a mixture of modes. The analytic group retains a woof of playfulness despite the fact that it is indeed serious business with a warp of important purpose. As in individual psychoanalysis there is deprivation or frustration as well as some kinds of gratification, and this balance of frustration and gratification is so adjusted that verbalization is encouraged, whereas direct actional satisfaction of hostile and sexual wishes is denied.

Group-analytic psychotherapy offers a contrast to the contrived experiences of other sorts of groups—encounter groups, confrontation groups, and marathon groups, some of which promote a variety of nonverbal exercises. Some of these contrived group experiences disregard—or at any rate minimize—the developmental continuity of sensation, feeling, and thought—and often enough and paradoxically—sequences of actual discontinuities and interactions that demand time for *working-through* and *integration* in therapy.

As in individual psychoanalysis there is a kind of monitoring of the emotional flow, an attempt on the part of the conductor to maintain and promote, if necessary, optimal amounts of affectively toned communication. This is but one aspect of the conductor's complex task, his discriminative role within the group whereby he safeguards it against unproductive regression. Such discriminative responsibility consists largely of verbal interpretations which become a part of each group member's activity by means of the learning alliance. Often when some manifestations of resistance—including specific defense mechanisms—are interpreted, communication can become more affectively toned, whereas when manifestations of transference longings are interpreted these often reduce excessive emotionality, some of which may be covert. Many kinds of transference reaction and interaction between one group member and another occur, and the consolidated transference of the group to the conductor and that of the members to the group are also to be taken into account. Interpreted, such transferences may make possible for group members the later retrospective reconstruction of childhood events, or it may stimulate recollection. Interpretation of the dominant theme to which group members are unconsciously responding may also be indicated. The work of interpretation is always to make the unconscious conscious as is appropriate for the group; its counterpart is the work of absorbing these interpretations and responding to them; this leads to *working-through* and eventual *integration.* All members of a group which is well under way as a progressively advancing analytic entity offer interpretations from time to time.

This essential aspect of group-analytic psychotherapy is described to emphasize its usefulness as a bulwark against excessive regression in the more expressive and emotionally releasing group activity. When the observing ego of group members is significantly diminished by acting, anti-therapeutic effects may result. When we visit the theater we are not only at a physical distance from the players but at a psychic distance too—as was the playwright himself. We see and hear those on the stage as though we were eavesdropping. Although we may become greatly excited and very much involved as the action unfolds, we generally return to some degree of psychic distance. This return depends on factors within ourselves, on the theme of the play, the techniques of the playwright and the director, and the skill of the actors. Although some productions recently have turned into forms of demonstration in which everyone participates, the invasion of the acting arena by an unduly excited audience comprising a mob is out of the question in the traditional theater, the rules of which are generally useful in promoting the enjoyment and profit of those in attendance, however inhibiting they may be in some respects.

In the complicated development of word language and phonetic symbolism from the image of the body, the organization of the ego is vastly enlarged and its capacity for conscious representation enormously increased (Abse, 1971). The deployment of word language does not *necessarily* disguise, conceal, or obstruct emotional responses. These may be given clearer form in expression, and may be better regulated. Besides, the tonal qualities of speech, the facial expressions of affect, and the other gestures that accompany words enrich meaning. Freud (1938) has shown that the inside of the ego, comprising thought processes, has the quality of being to a considerable extent preconscious. This preconscious territory of the ego is characterized by unobstructed access to consciousness, by its connections with the speech residues, and by a distinctive regulative (secondary) process. Group-analytic psychotherapy is an application of psychoanalysis that strives to increase this territory of the ego. It relies on the derepression and regression—insofar as these are regulated in the service of the ego.

PART IV

INNOVATIONS AND COMPARISONS

XVII Family Therapy

Family Life

IN 1921 Flugel suggested that if it is to some extent inevitable that children should come to regard their parents as obstacles to the full attainment of their own desires and unwelcome causes of interference with their most cherished activities, parents have at least equal reason to complain similarly of their children. There are, of course, bound to be sacrifices involved in active parenthood. The effort, responsibility, and anxiety involved in rearing children diminish very considerably the time and energy available for other occupations and ambitions. Indeed, Herbert Spencer saw an antagonism between individuation and propagation to be a general biologic law.

Conflicts of immediate interest between parents and children may not themselves be altogether negative in terms of furthering personal development. Indeed, in the long run, wisely moderated conflict of the family generations, including the living grandparents, may be quite positive in its developmental effects. In families in healthy homeostasis the conflicts of interest are in any case inset within and offset by an atmosphere of mutual enhancement of pleasure and of love. Not only are the nurturing and challenging parents the necessary personal environment for the development of the children, but, as Therese Benedek (1959) has expounded, parenthood can be a tremendous stimulus to further personal development of the parents themselves. On the negative side, however, the hostile feelings of parents toward their children which stem from resentment of sacrifice are often enormously amplified by the unconscious identification of the child with the parent's own parent (the child's grandparent). This tendency to identify a child with his grandparent in various ways is deeply implanted in the human mind. In fact, in many parts of the world grandparents are believed to be reincarnated in their grandchildren. This belief is basically responsible for the widespread practice of naming a child after a deceased grandparent, as when the eldest son is given the paternal grandparent's name.

Severely neurotic consequences in the family can follow a parent's unconscious identification of his child with his own violently hated father or mother. The affection which would be forthcoming from the parent for a particular child may thus be subverted, and this child may be left with an ambivalent fixation to the parent which is displaced to surrogate figures in later life. This may account, for example, for a love-craving unconsciously and intrinsically doomed to repeated guilty reenactment of a triangular drama, and a failure to achieve a stable pairing intimacy in adult life. For a person thus brought up in an atmosphere lacking in adequately sustained affection there is often an unconscious revenge motif which comes, disruptively, to expression in marriage, or which disrupts pairing relationship before marriage is begun or even contemplated.

As a vignette of this kind of interactive hostility in pairing, which is common (Nash et al., 1964), let me offer the case of a very talented young man who was repeatedly surprised and horrified when the young woman who was the current object of his conscious love and trust would become stormily hostile and terminate the erotic relationship with weeping and wailing. It became apparent in investigative psychotherapy that at the point of developing real commitment in a close relationship—a point reached repeatedly with a succession of young women—he would somehow become involved to some extent with another attractive young woman. Quite uncannily—as it seemed to him—a confrontation of the two demoiselles and a disrupted relationship would ensue, leaving him depressed and unable to work. Individual analytic work disclosed memories of being a show-piece for affluent young parents given to much party-going, who frequently left him in the care of coldly efficient baby-sitters. At certain times of intensified transference he assumed a flexed postural model on the couch, with clenched fists and grinding teeth. At other times he ashamedly recounted episodes that had occurred when he was five, of enticing a neighbor boy, about two-and-a-half years old, to the fence between their adjoining gardens, and beating on the little fingers with which the child clung to it until the child cried. Later analysis retrieved memories of himself at about two years of age, gripping the bars of his crib and clenching his jaws and crying as his parents left him for a party. It became clear that the ashamed sadistic memories of his behavior at the age of five were compounded of revengeful identifications with parental aggressors by whom he had felt tortured. As already briefly adumbrated, such revenge came also in more covert ways to infiltrate his attempts at pairing in later years. The early deprivation of adequate affection had come to overload his Oedipus complex with an increment of hostility and disturb his later erotic relationships with suitable young women.

Psychoneuroses are often disseminated from the families of the wealthy. Affluence in one generation may be associated with over-indulgence of children and a consequent failure to develop an adequate sense of responsibility. In the next generation immature parents delegate functions to an extent and in ways which are inimical to the healthy development of their children. Neurotic problems are generated whenever the emotional needs of children are ignored or minimized and the parents' impulses and drives consistently given precedence. Theodore Lidz (1967) lists under four rubrics the various interrelated functions of the family that foster the healthy development of children:

(1) The parental nurturant functions which must meet the child's needs and supplement his immature capacities in a different manner at each phase of his development.

(2) The dynamic organization of the family which forms the framework for the structuring and integration of the child's personality.

(3) The family as the primary social system in which the child learns the basic social roles, the value of social institutions, and the basic mores of society.

(4) The task of the parents and the family they create of transmitting to the child the essential instrumental techniques of the culture, including its language.

It is, of course, quite evident that adequacy of family functioning in regard to the needs of children is severely impaired when there is economic, social, and cultural deprivation. The extensive study of children of disorganized lower-class families reported by Eleanor Pavenstedt (1967) amply details the developmental arrests and deviations that are tragically engendered.

Alfred Adler (1917) was, as noted in Chapter I, originally responsible for initiating the practice of family-centered child guidance. In this way he transcended psychoanalysts' concentration on the particular relations of each patient to each of the members of his family in turn. He began to consider the mutual influences of the family as a structured whole, and the child in relation to his individual problems. As with some more recent theorists who have taken a family orientation, Adler fell into the pitfall of underestimating the forces of unconscious repressed infantile sexuality, including the Oedipus complex, but his "Individual Psychology" opened up a wide field for research by inquiring into the importance of birth order in conveying advantage or disadvantage for children.

He pointed out that the position of the oldest child precipitates a special problem. He is often for a considerable time the only child and is then dethroned. The oldest child frequently adopts a conservative point of view, believing that those in power should remain dominant. The second child has a tremendous urge to catch up. The youngest, of course, is in the position of an only child insofar as he is never dethroned by a successor. He lacks followers but has many pace-makers. Maintaining the view that the order of birth is powerfully influential and can be illustrated throughout human history, Adler points to several historical personages, Joseph among them. According to the Bible, Joseph was brought up as the youngest child. Benjamin came along 17 years after him and played no part in his early development. Joseph's style of life was typically that of a youngest child; he always asserted his superiority, even in his dreams, in which he outshone all others and accepted homage from them. He understood these dreams as prophecies, but to his brothers they were evidences of his arrogance. They felt threatened by him and plotted to get rid of him. However, from the position of being the last, and being excluded, Joseph rose to be the first, and the pillar and support of the whole family.

Yet, according to Adler (1927), youngest children are second only to oldest children in presenting problems. They are often over-indulged by all of the family, and may on that account never become adequately independent, easily losing courage while trying to succeed without support from others. Although youngest children are apt to be highly ambitious, they sometimes evince a laziness that comes from discouragement over the failure to attain their unrealistic exalted goals. It is easy to understand that feelings of gross inferiority lie beneath the inordinate ambition; the personal environment of the youngest child has been peopled for so long by his stronger and more experienced seniors.

Adler also describes the special problems of the only child, who is so often pampered by his mother that he develops excessive dependency upon her, and hatred of his father. He wants to be the center of attention all the time, and finds it difficult in later years also to be marginal even part of the time. The atmosphere of excessive parental anxiety about his welfare poses another threat to sound development. It was Adler's view that the position in the family left an indelible stamp on the life-style, and although the significance of birth order has been the subject of hundreds of publications since Galton's study of British scientists in 1874, no one has contributed as much as Adler, and most publications have confirmed and elaborated his clinical findings.

Zebulon Taintor (1970) recently offered the results of 323 psychiatric evaluations at a military recruit training camp, in which birth order is correlated with the likelihood of becoming a psychiatric patient. In this clinical study only children were found to be more likely than others to consult the military psychiatrist, to be diagnosed as psychoneurotic, and to be discharged from the service. The diagnoses of first children were almost equally divided between psychoneurosis and personality disorder, whereas few second children were diagnosed as being psychoneurotic and were preponderantly seen as having personality disorders.

The production of psychoneurotic symptoms depends in part on the presence of a lofty ego ideal or on a severely punitive primitive superego. First children tend to emulate their parents in an effort to please them. Second children, however, do not find this pathway open as they strive to be distinct from the older sibling. It seems that a sense of identity founded in part on negativism is more frequently encountered in a second or later child than in the first. Erik Erikson (1959) describes this phenomenon as the choice of the negative identity. Taintor gained the impression that the second child's development is often dictated by inner pressure to be different from his older sibling. However, if the parents had successfully transmitted to the first child the ideal of a studious, consistent, hardworking person, polite and interested in people, the second child may find that his departure from this standard does not please his parents. His self-esteem is thus lowered, and his potential for developing rebellious personality disorder may be raised. Taintor's investigation indicates the need for more research into the attitudes of parents to test such statistical statements as those indicating that parents lose interest in children beyond the first child. Such loss of interest would especially apply to middle children, who must experience the arrival of another baby who will attract what child-directed adult attention remains available. Adler had noted earlier that these middle children "had a dominant note of being neglected and slighted" (1927).

Hatred between siblings is an important factor in the pathogenesis of neurosis, as becomes clear in any discussion of the effect of birth order on individual character and destiny. Relationships with brothers and sisters are determinants second only to the complex relationships of the child with his parents. The hate components of the Oedipus complex are normal consequences of the intense love felt by the growing child toward the parent of the opposite sex, but hate toward the oncoming junior members of the family represents a more primary and prompt reaction. The claims of one sibling for the attention and affection of his parents come into conflict with the claims of the others. These claims and the conflicts they engender are only slightly less fierce than the exorbitant demands and related conflicts that characterize the Oedipus complex. The younger child also resents the advantages and privileges of the larger, stronger, more competent and more experienced older siblings to whom he must often submit. Older siblings, indeed, may be viewed as tyrants from whose tyranny relief can be obtained only through appeal to the parents or other adults who control the destinies of the very young. Group-analytic psychotherapy provides an opportunity to revisit and revise these sibling rivalries in the matrix of a group other than the family. The transference reactions that reveal themselves in this group are clarified and interpreted. It often becomes apparent also within an analytic group that much of the curiosity children show in regard to conception, gestation, and parturition arises from the connection of these events with the arrival of an intruder who threatens to deplete the available store of attention and affection, and of material supplies as well.

Psychotherapy of the family

In all its forms family therapy is based on an understanding of family pathogenetics and psychodynamics as they are revealed more and more in the process of verbal exchange, and on such appraisal of the family's strengths, limitations, and resources as can be made during the therapist's negotiation with its members. Important roots of neurotic maladaptations and psychotic disorder within the family have been already mentioned—inadequate parental affection and control, excessive hate responses on the part of the children, inadequate family structure, unfavorable position in the family constellation, and sibling jealousies—but there are others; and each would justify ample exposition in another context. When cultural deprivation is a factor this may disqualify family members for effective integration into society, although compensatory educational and socializing experiences may reduce the deficiency (Pavenstedt, 1967). Another sort of cultural deprivation is evident in the family in which the children have moved into a more sophisticated world than the one in which the parents remain. The family therapist identifies distortions in a pathogenic family style of communication, and works toward their correction. When a congenital physical handicap is a factor its psychic ramifications may require special remedial work, and psychotherapy for all family members may be necessary for the therapeutic modification of the ways in which they respond to the one who is afflicted.

All types of family therapy work with the natural group, and not with the individual patient as in psychoanalysis, or with a contrived collection of patients as in group-analytic psychotherapy. Although in some types of family therapy the therapist may spend some psychotherapeutic time with selected family members, in *family conjoint therapy* he reproduces the situation defined by Virginia M. Satir (1966) as one in which disturbed persons are treated in the family units to which they currently belong, and deals with the interactions of all in each psychotherapeutic session.

Customarily, one family member regarded as "sick" will be identified as the patient, whereas other family members may be disturbed in a variety of ways and in varying degrees. The family therapist faces the cluster of interpenetrating attitudes held by family members, and cannot profitably concentrate on "the patient" alone. After interviewing the patient he will ask the whole family to "come in and talk things over", since they are all affected one way or another, however adequately they have managed to adapt socially without manifesting sickness.

After initial observation of family interaction, the therapist tries to foster among the family members a climate conducive to freer and more significant communication. He supports each who tries to make himself understood, either by the therapist himself or by the ones in the family with whom he has been at odds. The therapist capitalizes on the matrix of the first family session, in which his charismatic aura of special skill in understanding and healing has given authority and promise. His presence *vis-à-vis* the group challenges the *status quo*, and galvanizes its collective will-to-health. From time to time he makes interpretations that deflate defensive postures, remove disguises, and clarify the prevailing situation, obviating confusion and misunderstanding. Typical defensive communications contain projection, displacement, rationalization, denial, reaction formations, repressive forgettings, and separation of affect from ideation. Such defensive communications are partly in collision and partly in collusion.

Tactful exploration of these defenses is necessary if they are to be overcome. The therapist moves only gradually toward exposing and clarifying problems, and his progress usually evokes emotional turbulence and exacerbates overt hostility. Open interactional expression is given to hitherto dormant or concealed interpersonal conflicts. Although one must break eggs to make an omelet, the good cook keeps them all cooking together so that the finished dish has integrity of consistency! Intra- as well as inter-personal conflict may from time to time be elucidated by the therapist, who concerns himself especially with the recognition and discussion of scape-goating patterns that fortify any family member at the expense of another. He seizes every opportunity, in this as in other psycho-therapeutic contexts, to reduce that neurotic guilt which underlies the need to suffer.

The conversion of disguised and repressed conflict to open quarreling creates significant strain and threatening disruption. The support provided by the therapist is the only means by which such strain can be modified and endured. This phase of family therapy is prolonged, and it may easily become excessively stormy. Ackerman (1966) urges that the therapist assume the role of a strong parent figure and controller of interpersonal danger, and offer a source of emotional support and satisfaction that will provide "emotional elements that the family needs but lacks". This kind of substitution therapy, he believes, demands that the therapist display more appropriate images for family relationship than family members have previously entertained.

Don Jackson and Gregory Bateson (1956) described the *double bind phenomenon* characteristic of families in which one or more persons were identified as schizophrenic. The double bind conveys, by either verbal or nonverbal means, simultaneous directives for two kinds of diametrically opposed behavior. For example, a parent who upholds parental authority may, often quite unconsciously, be signaling his child to rebel. Double binds of less significance can be seen even in the family without any clinical manifestation of schizophrenia, as when one parent insists on traditional values and the other actively supports avant-garde views. A split of this kind puts a double bind on a susceptible child inasmuch as he cannot please both his parents at once and is thus immobilized. The recognition and discussion of the double bind, as well as of other types of communication distortion, are essential in family therapy.

In recent years some psychotherapists have used the videotape confrontation in individual and group therapy. Milton M. Berger (1971, 1972) and Ian Alger* (1971) experimented with its use in family therapy. Videotape can be particularly useful in focusing on ambiguous messages and faulty communication, especially on their nonverbal kinesic components. Television may be a useful adjunct to therapy by providing an opportunity to view the human encounter of a session. For example, hysterical women patients can behave in an inappropriately seductive and flirtatious way without being aware of this or providing modifying signals. Alger described one patient's embarrassed recognition, on playback, that her behavior had been unsuitably flirtatious, with thigh exposure and breast thrusting; in subsequent sessions she caught herself and gave countervailing signals. A videotape confrontation in family therapy also stimulates the renewal, from a more objective point of view than before, of the discussion of events that occurred during the therapeutic session.

If an individual is to change, it is frequently necessary for the context in which he lives to change, especially in families of low socio-economic class. In such a case the patient is in a massive double bind; he may become seriously sick if separated from his family, but in the family he is part of the sickness. Since he cannot be extricated from the family soup, the soup must be doctored. I have thought of such patients as "aliquots"; they are contained in the family and divide into it without a remainder. Their basic individuation and socialization are insufficient; the collective family dependency is too deep. Individual therapy in such cases offers only the temporary abatement of symptoms, as does group therapy in a group not composed of family members. For this reason family

* Alger and Hogan reported to the 24th Annual Conference of the American Group Psychotherapy Association in 1967 on the impact of videotape recording on insight in group psychotherapy.

therapy is a particularly important treatment modality in the community mental health clinic.

The disadvantages are many, however, when it is compared with group-analytic therapy undergone by similarly situated patients striving energetically to get out of the family soup. We have noted how important it is to monitor the emotional flow and to keep it at an optimal level so that excessive emotionality displayed by a patient does not preclude his acquisition of insight, nor does any inadequacy of his affective expression keep him from emotional realization. Excessive storminess in therapy as the defenses are interpreted frequently cannot be reduced adequately by transference interpretation in family therapy, yet if the defenses are not dealt with they remain consolidated against the expression of affect. It is indeed remarkable that ingenious and innovative family therapists are able in considerable measure to overcome these impediments and to catalyze substantial socio-adaptive progress in the family.

The problems of family therapy highlight the advantages of using group-analytic therapy when feasible. The judicious grouping of strangers whose private lives are not mutually involved facilitates interpretation of transferences that develop. Emotionality is adequate much of the time for the purposes of working-through and integrating the experiences in the group. The fear of perishing without the family, the sheer need to survive with them, does not block adequate verbalization in the group of strangers to the same extent as it often does initially in the family gathering, in which it is sometimes necessary for the therapist to be highly active, and on occasion even evangelical. One thinks of Milton's lines:

> What in me is dark
> Illumine, what is low raise and support;
> That to the height of this great argument
> I may assert eternal Providence
> And justify the ways of God to man.*

* *Paradise lost.*

Group-analytic therapy was designed to prevent impediments to analysis, which is the reaching out from the here-and-now to disturbances in the past with which the patient is unconsciously burdened in the present. In this psychoanalytic sense, family therapy presents greater difficulties; feelings arising in therapy are expressed and examined with the very people who provoked them and with whom life-space is shared from day to day. The patient certainly cannot expect the same immunity from retaliation as that provided in group-analytic therapy. This lack of immunity is, however, sometimes not disadvantageous to a socio-adaptive approach to treatment. As John Weakland (1962) indicated, in family therapy the object of the patient's anger may come to understand the reason for this anger and to make overtures toward reconciliation. Certainly, the extent to which the patient benefits from family therapy depends enormously on the personality of the therapist, especially his warmth. The importance of the therapist's personality in all psychotherapies has been emphasized by such writers as Hans Strupp (1960); it is notably crucial in family therapy.

Group psychotherapy for married couples is a configuration of considerable interest since it is, in effect, an outgrowth of both family therapy and therapy with a group of strangers. When it is conducted with analytic goals it often lends itself to an analytic mode of group therapy.

Psychiatrists in clinical practice frequently see patients whose presenting symptoms are the immediate result of neurotic interaction with the spouse. Symptom-producing or symptom-revealing neurotic interactions may relate to all areas of their life together, or uniquely to one, which is often the *vita sexualis*. Therapy groups are sometimes composed of three or four such patients, along with their spouses. Anthony Gottlieb and E. Mansel Pattison (1966) brought into focus one aspect of this interaction which is also highly important in marriage counseling. They reported that in the early phases of a group in psychotherapy, typical interactive patterns were blocked by the marital relationship. The natural couples displayed a "pairing defense", with couples talking to couples and one spouse speaking for the other as though they were one. At this stage the group protocol resembled one designed for four persons instead of the eight actually taking part. Presently, however, following the early demand to be treated as a unit, resentment arose when one spouse presumed to speak for the other. It also became customary later to retreat to this early unitary identity during times of anxiety about differences between husband and wife. The pairing defense was also manifest in the fear that involvement with other members might become sexual, or mean the loss of one's spouse to another member. It was, however, amenable to therapeutic intervention, which was followed by the development of typical marital interaction patterns between husband and wife, with the coping styles of each marriage becoming evident. As therapy progressed the couples had less need to retreat to a "smothering, exclusive, unhappy symbiosis". As the need to preserve this actually dys-symbiotic oneness diminished, the four couples became eight people and began to display typical patterns of behavior toward their respective spouses and then toward other group members of the opposite sex. As Gottlieb and Pattison reported:

> Then a man (or woman) was seen to relate to the other women (or men) just as he did to his own wife, with all the same unrealistic expectations and defensive behavior. For example, Dan D. talked to Barbara B. and accused her of wanting him to fail, to which Barbara replied: "Why should I want you to fail? You act just as if I were your wife."

Of course, living as a human being is enriched by a certain flexibility of association with and disassociation from others. Patients like those described come to understand only with difficulty that the periodic closeness of the marriage relationship, particularly intense in sexual intercourse, does not necessitate the denial of the many differences between a man and a woman, as neurotic anxiety may dictate. Neurotic anxiety and denial concerning these differences can result in a profound threat to the process of individuation and in a threat to sexual identity at various phases of the life cycle. In avoiding neurotic anxiety by denial the individual becomes imperiled by engulfment. He (or she) then protests against this, with ensuing marital storms and tensions.

In analytic group treatment the patients are eventually enabled to achieve more adequate and secure individuation and flexibility.

Peter Blos (1962) has refined our knowledge of problems of individuation and ego synthesis as they occur throughout normal as well as deviant adolescent development. Individual psychotherapy is apt quickly to arouse primitive dependency–independency conflicts of great emotional intensity in the disturbed adolescent, who all too often flees from treatment. When several such adolescents are treated in a group, the partial mutual absorption of their dependency needs diminishes their resistance to the psychotherapeutic process. Nevertheless, other severe problems may soon surface in the group, notably strong sibling rivalry transference reactions which disrupt group cohesion, or an exaggeratedly defiant coalition of peers which can result in uncontrollable acting-out and produce chaos rather than therapeutic gain. However, the group method is frequently beneficial, even for delinquent youths, in an institutional setting. Adolescent group therapy in an institution is most effective when it takes place in the context of a therapeutic community—one in which the adolescent patients share in decision-making. In such a situation, and with appropriate monitoring, the group therapy process is often ego-building; it can improve social adaptation and facilitate the necessary taming of affect. During much of the time the leader-therapist of such a group must focus on current and specific topics of group discussion. More intelligent and more verbal older adolescents can often be treated better in a more analytic group approach; or two may be treated together in a group of adults undergoing group-analytic psychotherapy.

Adolescent turmoil is often to a considerable extent the result of disintegrative influences at work in a sick or broken family. Anxiety, doubt, and distrust may characterize the family life, and adequate affection may be lacking. There may be no patterns for cooperation and functional differentiation, and family stability may be in daily jeopardy, with conflict rather than harmonious neutrality the rule. Under such conditions an adolescent's behavioral disturbance not only betrays his deviant personality but points to family disorder. In the case of one 16-year-old girl who repeatedly ran away from an "infantilizing" mother and an alcoholic father, it was clear that the key did not lie in individual therapy. The father, usually withdrawn and depressed while sober, became either violent or given to indiscriminate sexual mauling in his cups. The mother, who had recently turned away from her daughter, demanded that she become independent. The couple, married for 20 years, had given up sexual intercourse 10 years earlier because of their progressively developing interactive hostility.

Adolescent turmoil in such a context may yield more quickly to family therapy when the therapist is able to secure the cooperation of the other family members, to lend stability to the family unit by his support, and, in due course, to indicate that responsibility for the illness is shared within the family; and when he can counter and analyze the denials and projections that could otherwise be used to justify the expulsion of the patient, perhaps to a hospital, as the only "bad ingredient" in the family soup.

The home visit is no more fashionable in this country in the practice of psychiatry than it is in medical practice in general, but a question about the value of family therapy conducted in the home has recently been raised. Alfred S. Friedman (1970), in an important contribution, has given an account of a therapy team's efforts with a number of families seen in their respective homes. Each family was having difficulty with a schizophrenic adolescent. The use of the family home as the setting for family therapy has disadvantages and complications, but the advantages may outweigh them. This is an important field for investigation, and one with incidental implications for the therapist's own feelings of power and authority. The treatment of a natural group *in situ* may threaten him as well as some of the family members. Some therapists may feel that their prestige is reduced by going to the family rather than having the family come to them, and that further uncertainties are thus introduced into the situation.

XVIII Group Therapy and Gestalt

PLATO was familiar with one of the oldest psychological theories, and Aristotle later formulated it in much the same language as that found in modern psychology texts. This theory attempts to account for all thought and conduct on the basis of laws of association, of which there are two according to Aristotle: the law of *similarity* (or opposition or contrast); and the law of *contiguity*. The first states that one idea tends to call up another that resembles or opposes it. For example, when a small boy is told that the earth is spheroidal he may think of an orange, and later come to use the simile "round like an orange". On the other hand, if asked to react immediately to the word "black" he might say "white". The second law, the law of *contiguity*, states that one idea tends to follow another if the two ideas had previously been experienced together in time, either simultaneously or successively. James Mill (1829) illustrated the second law in this fashion:

> I see a horse: that is a perception. Immediately I think of his master: that is an idea, arising out of previously seeing him on the horse's back. Then the idea of his master makes me think of his office, he is minister of state: that is another idea arising out of seeing him functioning as such. The idea of a minister of state arouses thoughts of public affairs, and a train of political ideas ensues.

Associationism in its simplest form describes the human being as an elaborate machine that responds to the environment in causally determined ways, and behaviorism implicitly makes the same assumptions. Both schools of thought have been considerably modified and elaborated, the latter recently with concepts derived from cybernetics in terms of both feed-forward and feed-back mechanisms, as in the theory of operant conditioning. The conditioning concepts, insofar as they resist integration into wider contexts of thought, establish a robot image of man. Moreover, largely as a result of fascination with data-processing machinery, models of simplified cognitive functioning, divorced from the affective and conative bases of mentation, have been constructed, and foster an image of man as being very much like a computer. Thus a partitive account describes man as being on the one hand a system of reflexes, and on the other an electronic digital and analogue computer. Even taken together, the two notions do not add up to a picture of man as a sentient and creatively adapting human being.

In a development of simple associationism and conditioning, Freud and William McDougall (1923) both emphasized that the prime movers are those instinctual pressures which, interacting with deep cognitive structures, prod and steer the human mind from within. Modern views, largely indebted to psychoanalysis and hormic psychology, as well as to gestalt psychology, have enlarged the perspective; we see the human mind as being intrinsically active both in "the here and now" and in maturation and development.

According to the simplest form of associationism, sensory responses to the environment are linked so that sensations acquire meaning and become percepts. These percepts eventually give rise to ideas linked together passively and mechanically according to the laws of similarity (and contrast) and contiguity. In this view, the infant first sees the world as a blurring, booming confusion, as William James (1890) imagined, and it is only gradually that some parts of this world take on meaning for him in terms of pleasure and pain, and attraction and avoidance; and later he generates thought in association with particular faces and recalled images.

Stress by gestalt psychologists on the perceptual factor in learning has modified this simple scheme in much careful experimentation. To illustrate: an animal is trained to find his food in the darker of two gray boxes; the box painted in the lighter shade of gray is then replaced by a third box of a darker color than the "food-box"; the animal now turns to this one for his reward, demonstrating that he has learned to respond to the light–dark pattern rather than to a specific shade of gray, and that his response pertains to larger patterns or configurations—*gestalten*—rather than to separate stimuli.

Max Wertheimer (1912, 1925) and Wolfgang Köhler (1925, 1929), the gestalt psychologists, were led by their experiments and observations with animals and humans to believe that the perceptual process is always one of active organization of configurations, of picking out a figure from its ground, of grouping stimuli and making patterns, according to laws that not only are congruent with those of Aristotle but that enrich our understanding of these classic formulations. This pattern-making reflects basic isomorphic brain dynamics. The baby does *not* see the world as a blurring confusion but, when his eyes function, comes to see his mother's face as a configuration, a *gestalt*, because of the innate structure and function of the visual centers and association pathways in the brain. Of course, the baby's experience leads to extension of meaning, but the building blocks are not separate stimuli; they are organized patterns of already organized sensations, with sensory feedback from associated organized motor responses.

Köhler found that when his chimpanzees could see their food at the end of an obstructed pathway they took an appropriate roundabout open path, without resort to trial-and-error learning. All the elements of the situation being visible, the animal grasped the total pattern and solved the problem immediately. A banana placed outside the chimpanzee's cage out of reach but attached to a string that hung within reach was immediately hauled in by means of the string. The chimpanzee made occasional mistakes due to the initial complexity of visual pattern when several strings, only one of which was attached to the out-of-reach banana, were dangled before him; but in a large series of trials with several different chimpanzees the operative strings were pulled much sooner than the probability of blind trial-and-error would indicate. When a banana hung out of reach before the cage and a stick was available in the back of the cage, chimpanzees did not immediately use the stick as a tool to obtain the prize. In the absence of a compact visual pattern the "gap" in the situation was at first too wide to be instantly bridged. However, when the stick was placed in full view near the banana it was readily employed, and later, even when it had been left at the back of the cage, it was put to profitable use. Observation of such behavior led Köhler to hypothesize that the ape's solution of the problem of getting a banana did not take place only as an incident in varied motor responses—as postulated by trial-and-error learning theories—but also as a result of sudden insight which took place in the field of perceptual organization whenever the conditions of the experiment permitted.

Incidentally, city planners might profitably bear in mind that certain of the frustrations involved in trial-and-error learning, and the irritation and psychophysiologic tensions thereby produced, could be largely prevented by urban design informed by gestalt principles; John Citizen could more often and more conveniently get his version of the banana if compact and significant patterns were provided to facilitate perceptual organization and discrimination.

In gestalt principles of organization the law of similarity—the counterpart of Aristotle's law of association—indicates that similar items (for example, those alike in form and color) or similar transitions (those alike in the steps separating them) tend to form groups in perception. The law of proximity, as the gestalt psychologists call it—the counterpart of Aristotle's other law of association by *contiguity*—indicates that perceptual grouping is favored according to the nearness of the parts. Other important principles are derived from gestalt studies: the law of *closure* indicates that closed areas are more stable than unclosed ones and therefore form figures in perception more readily; and the law of *continuation* indicates that perceptual organization tends to occur in such a manner that a broken straight line appears to continue as a straight line, a partial circle as a circle, and so on, even though many other kinds of perceptual structuring would be possible. *Closure* and *continuation* are aspects of articulate organization. In accordance with these principles a major function of the perceptual apparatus turns out to be the stripping away of redundant stimulation and the encoding of incoming information in an economical form useful for the organism. Organismically, perception is governed by the law of *prägnanz*, which provides that when patterns of stimuli offer many possible interpretations, the one most economical and useful to the organism at that time will be selected. Gestalt psychologists offer many figures to illustrate the principles adumbrated, among then the widely known and classical ambiguous pattern shown here.

After Rubin (1915)

Although gestalt theory originated in studies of perception, its critical hypotheses—emphasis on the whole as more than the sum of its parts, and the reciprocal roles of the part and the whole—came to influence ways of looking at data in psychology in general and in clinical psychology in particular. For example, in working with severely brain-damaged victims of World War I, Kurt Goldstein (1939) came to understand their urgent need to deny their functional disturbance in their attempt to maximize their capacity to deal with any given situation. He noted that the brain damage impaired the "abstract attitude" and led to concrete response in all situations, even those in which an abstract—or a dominantly abstract—attitude was demanded. In contrast, the healthy, undamaged individual is able to shift from one attitude to another at will, and to adjust creatively to whichever the total situation requires.

Kurt Lewin (1936), who applied the technique of topology to problems of goal-directed behavior, was originally associated with Köhler in Berlin. He believed that the physically and socially structured field within which an individual lives and moves—his life-space—can be represented by topological figures. He proceeded to apply field theory to the study of small-group dynamics. In 1946 he attended a conference initiated by the Connecticut Interracial Commission for the purpose of fostering local leadership that would help communities to understand and to comply with the Fair Employment Practices Act. There were three ten-member groups, composed for the most part of teachers and social workers. Under Lewin's guidance each group had a research observer who, in separate evening sessions, reported the patterns of interaction he had seen. Some of the participants in the ten-member daily discussion groups unexpectedly asked to attend these evening research meetings, and they were allowed to do so. The discussions of their own behavior and its consequences had an electrifying effect on them, and they began to join the observers and leaders in trying to analyze and interpret the events of each daily meeting in which they took part. This effort provided significant insights into their own behavior and that of the group; thus a potentially powerful medium of reeducation had revealed itself.

Shortly thereafter the National Training Laboratories was formed to develop a method of learning by simultaneous participation in and observation of a group. Its extended program at Bethel, Maine, now includes not only problems of community conflict but the application of the method to industrial management, educational advancement, and personal growth. The time format of the National Training Laboratories is typically that of an extended workshop, ranging from three days to several weeks, during which two-hour sessions are conducted several times a day.

Group-analytic psychotherapy has attempted to integrate both psychoanalytic and gestalt viewpoints within the conductor's task of understanding and clarifying—whenever clarification serves a therapeutic purpose—the events that occur during group sessions. Thus the conductor is attentive to the level of events that forms the theme for the group as a whole. For example, the theme of failure, emasculation, and humiliation may arise, only to be suddenly interrupted by general withdrawal from further investigation—or elaborative discussion. Withdrawal may be indicated by a general silence, by a change of topic, or, perhaps, by a turn to more superficial conversation that is supportive and couched in "the language of social cohesion". In another example, the conductor might note and comment on the high level of pervasive anxiety, and on those indications that it has been provoked by the absence of a member. It may become evident that one member is playing the role of a rebellious son to another's depiction of a ruthlessly castigating father, and by commenting on this the conductor may be able to increase the awareness of interpersonal events in the group. Again, a member might verbalize more or less adequately the substance of intrapsychic conflict, an example of which would be the discussion of sexual wishes in the past and feelings of guilt because what he had desired had in that place and time been forbidden. In group-analytic psychotherapy one pattern that emerges from the "ground" of individual events may gradually be focused upon and regarded by the conductor as a "figure" of concern to all. Thus, individual intrapsychic or interpersonal events may become the "figure" and more general events the "background", or vice versa. Just as the ambiguous figure illustrated can be seen first as a chalice and then as facing human profiles, so may the group events arrange themselves—without intrinsic change—into changing patterns, in some of which the figure is the group as a whole, and in others of which the figure will be the interaction of the individual members with one another.

These changing perceptual attitudes are creatively adjusted to the therapeutic task at any particular moment in the group process. The conductor of group-analytic psychotherapy participates within the group in a manner that is both discriminative and flexible, in contrast to the rigid outside stance adopted by a leader in the kind of group analysis advocated by Wilfred R. Bion (1961). According to Bion, the leader's task is limited to focusing attention on immediate intra-group tensions; their investigation constitutes the group's assignment. Thus the focus engendered differs among various kinds of analytic groups, although both psychoanalytic and gestalt principles may be employed in each.

Bion's language is ambiguous and apt to mislead, but he is clear enough in his belief that each group tends to adopt an emotional state. He insists that whatever the avowed purpose or task of a group may be, it will soon be accompanied and sometimes even eclipsed by whatever emotional state so pervades the membership that each group can be called "a basic assumption group". For example, primitive dependency strivings may predominate—or an alertness to fight or flight; or members may become hopefully preoccupied with pairing. Margaret Rioch (1970) has written an admirable, albeit uncritical, summary of Bion's work, and offers a useful clarification of his ideas.

The leader dedicated to Bion's theory and its practice will focus on the group as a whole dynamic field, possibly seeing it at times in relation to other organized fields. He will exclude the individual's characteristics and dyadic relationship from his interpretive interventions except insofar as his comments might identify them as a threat to the focus on group events. This one-sidedness itself provokes tension among the group members but it does highlight some patterns of group functioning.

This method contrasts with that pioneered by Frederick Perls (1969), who appropriated the term "gestalt therapy" to describe his procedures. Perls did in fact conduct individual therapy within the group, although his therapy was informed by gestalt principles.

He always sat, flanked by two empty chairs, at one end of the room in which his group met. One of the chairs was "the hot seat", reserved for anyone desirous of coming forward to work. The other was left vacant to help the working patient to dramatize the alienated parts of himself as, with the help of the leader, they were recovered. At an appropriate point in the interaction with the patient Perls would have him change seats in order to externalize a heretofore dissociated but now recovered image of himself, and to promote further awareness of it by acting. At another point the patient would be directed to confront one group member after another in order to experience whatever attitude or feeling he had been discussing. This "going around" sometimes entailed the acting-out of the previously suppressed opposite of some habitual behavior pattern, with a customarily ingratiating person acting in aggressive self-assertion, for example, perhaps putting into action newly achieved maturity in relating to other people. Fellow members of the group would be encouraged, but not required, to respond.

As director-manager, Perls would induce the patient in "the hot seat" to make a part of himself alive in that moment of time, and the intensity with which this would be carried out led other group members to vicarious participation in the interaction being observed. The identifications and resonances of the participants in Perls's workshops came from his insistence on bringing every experience vividly into the here-and-now and his encouragement of the group's use of itself as an instrument for the benefit of the individual. Talk about the past was disparaged as mere gossip, and the past was presented immediately and directly instead, as when a young man, rambling on about his childhood experience with his mother, was directed to play it out instead, and to take the role of the boy and the mother alternately. This procedure often resulted in what Perls called "explosions"—massive abreactions or breakthroughs of intense feeling.

Perls's work, like that of some of his disciples, makes use of some of the most significant insights of gestalt psychology. He clarified and defined his vision of the "figure", picking it out from its ground and interpreting its coherence or split in terms of the context of the actual situation. He attempted in these ways to foster self-awareness and to promote the assumption of responsibility. Perls did not, however, accept the term *unconscious* nor fully accept the concept it represents, substituting instead those unrealized aspects of behavior that he considered either unavailable or only potentially present.

This brief discussion of the methods of Bion and Perls indicates that each stultifies freedom of interaction in group therapy in different ways, whereas in group-analytic therapy such freedom is fostered to a point short only of acting-out. The freedom of verbal interaction in group-analytic psychotherapy permits also the exploration of the past. Important as the exploration of the here-and-now is in all group work, it is, after all, the repressed past which is the predominant creator of pathology. Freud's simile of the mummy which falls to dust when finally unearthed remains cogent.

XIX Problems of Encounter Groups

THE extraordinary proliferation of encounter and sensitivity groups during the past five years has created hazards and problems. All too often we have had to deal clinically with the fallout from such groups—people with exacerbated neuroses or sudden psychotic decompensation. Such clinical experience, along with some theoretical issues raised by our work with group-analytic groups, necessarily influences our attitudes toward the "small-group movement".

Although there are many different kinds of encounter groups—sensory awareness groups, marathon groups, human relations groups, personal potential groups, psychological karate groups, and so on—with as many formats—they all have in common the goal of provoking their members to intense emotional experience. The leaders of each insist on rapid self-revelation, and focus on the here-and-now. There is some range in specific emphasis among the various types. Many promise the peak experience of joy—an ecstatic "turning-on"—and work eagerly for this exciting form of release. Others stress learning how to become "open" to a full appreciation of life's possibilities, and to the ungrudging sharing of life.

One can only sympathize with these goals, two sides of the same coin. The world does seem at times dull and commonplace; it is tempting to think of escape from its limitations. In *The social basis of consciousness* Burrow declared that man was severed by his self-awareness from the stream of life designed to engulf him and sweep him along, and his views can be seen dramatized in the works of D. H. Lawrence, the novelist, who agreed with him

(1927). Burrow and his co-workers tried persistently to counter within a small group—and within themselves—the affects and prejudices of habitual response, and to relieve inner tensions by breaking their shells and joining mankind in a solidarity of common feeling. The encounters and conflicts in Lawrence's novels take place at emotional and sensual levels, replacing the more conventional socially-determined interplay that provided dramatic tension for his contemporaries. Lawrence faced his readers with a unitary view of life, and broke many taboos with his appreciation of the cogency of sensuality and the use of sexuality as a binding agent and challenge in human relatedness. His characters exemplify the unselfconscious freedom the loss of which Burrow mourned and struggled to overcome. The loving innocence each of these men envisioned is the goal of most of today's encounter groups, and commands respect. The short cuts toward its attainment offered by some group work parody Burrow's effort, however, and the anti-intellectual position into which he and Lawrence were to some extent forced by their obsession with it needs examination. As long as his words make compelling music the poet-prophet gives little offense when he shrugs at mind, but the medical scientist who denies mind as an instrument with which to explore both inner and outer darkness does offend.

It is usual enough to see patients who have retreated in their neuroses into a one-sided intellectuality that defends against sexuality, confines them to a world of symbolic abstraction, and deprives them of the warmth of human closeness; but it is also usual to see patients whose search for another dimension through the group experience has created equally stringent limitations of another kind, and comparable emotional poverty.

For the most part—although not always—encounter groups foster the illusion that beneficial change can be accomplished without pain, and that heightened joy is the key to the new Kingdom of Heaven. Often they encourage also an extraordinary disregard for the network of personal relationships and responsibilities that preexists this venture; responsibility toward one's dependent children is sometimes considered altogether secondary to "fulfillment", for example. Patients who have been repeatedly exposed to the encounter-group experience seem to have retreated to shallow and changeable love relationships in which a spurious insistence on honesty scarcely conceals the underlying self-indulgence and irresponsibility. It is as though the developmental view of life with its sequential unfolding and advance is disregarded in favor of an indefinitely prolonged and indulged adolescence, sure not only to compromise the grasp of reality but to arouse deep-seated and dissociated feelings of guilt.

Our sympathy with the desire for more abundant life makes the casualties of such an understandable search seem all the more pathetic. They are torn by exacerbated guilts and anxieties, and sometimes even driven by their group experiences into disastrous and irreversible life situations; we cannot agree that the casualties who subsequently bring their disappointment to a psychiatrist are the only casualties. There is no doubt that the impact of a group can be tremendously useful in reducing the *need for suffering*, providing the work is not unduly hastened. We have found that when too much is attempted too soon in this direction a temporary dissociation of the severely punitive superego is all that is effected. Backlash and profoundly depressive reactions can then be expected to follow and even to lead some few participants to suicide unless there is psychiatric intervention.

One might answer such criticism by pointing to the firmly held belief that reorganization follows disorganization, and that there is reason to anticipate that such reorganization will proceed along healthy lines. It is impossible, however, to overlook the fact that efforts to change human beings too much too fast are dangerous. Responsible psychotherapy strives for gradual progressive change rather than overnight alteration, and takes into consideration the degree of disorganization best calculated to maximize sound psychic reorganization. It also allows for accompanying disruptions in reality, the careful screening of candidates, and the obtaining of informed consent in all practices. Many popular group programs are far less fastidious.

In their study of the casualties of group encounter Irving Yalom and Morton Lieberman (1971) identify one type of leader they consider contributory. He is forceful, authoritarian, intrusive, and aggressive, and well endowed with charisma. Impatient for dramatic signs of change (weeping, testimonials, breakdown, or breakthrough), he is persistent in challenging and facing the members of his group. He operates on a system of immediate gratification and pays little attention to *working-through* his patients' difficulties. He disregards individual differences among his patients, and seems to believe that their needs are all alike and their potentials similar.

After all, not everyone needs to express himself more vigorously and spontaneously, to shuck his societal restrictions, to achieve a greater degree of freedom, to abandon all success-oriented goals. Some individuals may need quite the opposite; they already express themselves with far too much lability; they need more, not fewer controls, they need more, not less of an ego boundary; they need, perhaps, a more structured, more traditionally based hierarchy of values.

The most vulnerable group members in the Yalom and Lieberman study were those with low self-esteem and unrealistically high expectation of the change they might expect to undergo in 30 hours of group experience. These are high risk patients for the especially stimulating and intrusive leader to deal with.

No one disputes that when group members introject the narcissistically invested and sometimes idealized image of the leader, this introject helps the patient to become less rigid, to "hang loose" instead of "being uptight". He becomes more tolerant of his own needs and wishes, and more flexible through his identification with his therapist, gaining something also by sharing the orientation of others in the group who may be more socially realistic than himself. In group-analytic psychotherapy the craving for magic and those intense transferences that make the group leader the parent are interpreted when appropriate, and made understandable little by little. In a sound and gradual way what is offered by the conductor and by fellow members succeeds in modifying the more primitive punitive aspects of the member's archaic superego. Group-analytic psychotherapy offers other advantages that encounter groups do not: the maintenance of an emotional level that allows for adequate ventilation without imperiling the observing ego; opportunities to bring the past to life through transference; and enough time—typically, in regular weekly sessions for more than a year—to work through conflictual material verbally, and to arrive at insight. These ingredients of the therapeutic process interact in effecting both symptomatic improvement and "self-realization".

Rapidly uncovering (derepressive) methods of group analysis are unsuitable for the brief treatment of neurotic problems. In some encounter groups the first stage of the rapid demolition of defense is followed by a short middle interval in which acting-out takes place, accompanied by grossly inadequate working-through, and abrupt faulty termination becomes inevitable (page 41). The way in which group-analytic psychotherapy terminates is a critical determinant of each patient's memories and, indeed, of his subsequent course. Undesirable consequences ensue whenever the "mourning" that characterizes the ending of the experience is too brief, or is either ignored or denied. Such an impending separation provides a golden opportunity for advantageous working-through of a profoundly important aspect of human relatedness. Moreover, failure to use the separation as a therapeutic exercise can aggravate pathology where it might reduce it, and inhibit growth where it might foster it. A typical clinical example will illustrate . . .

A twice-married woman in her mid-thirties came for individual analysis because of periodic long-lasting depressions and frequent headaches. For five years she had sought to relieve her loneliness by participation in a variety of encounter groups; she made the acquaintance in them of several men with whom to pair briefly and to have sexual intercourse. When each group came to an abrupt end she felt exhilarated at first, but shortly plunged again into feelings of despair.

She had been her father's indulged favorite until she was seven years old, when he began to drink heavily and neglected his family. He absconded with a mistress when the patient was 11. Five years later her mother married a man whom the girl greatly admired, seeking and finding favor in his eyes. The stepfather died suddenly of coronary thrombosis when she was 20. Shortly thereafter she married, and enjoyed a reasonably happy life for five years until her husband was killed in an automobile accident.

By then she had borne two children. Three years later she married a "confirmed bachelor" five years her senior, who was conscientious and dedicated, if somewhat rigid. After a few years her new husband became more relaxed and considerably more expressive emotionally; he was a devoted father to her children. She felt unable to trust him, however, and was unhappy over what she described as her "uncanny" lack of response, and began to experience headaches, periodic attacks of depression, and occasional intense feelings of loneliness. It was then—five years before undertaking analysis—that she discovered the group experience, with which she became fascinated, repeating it as often as possible—at least a half-dozen times in different geographical locations.

In analysis she came to see these group experiences and the brief pairing involvements as a reenactment of the childhood family drama that had culminated in abandonment, the reaction to which had been reinforced by the subsequent abrupt termination of other experiences of closeness and the traumas of a hot-and-cold love life. Her addiction to encounter groups contained an effort to obtain mastery by means of compulsive repetition. This motive might have been engaged usefully in a genuinely therapeutic analytic group experience that analyzed and respected defenses, and provided time for the working-through of loss and separation anxiety, allowing her to learn to relate well to her husband and children. Such an outcome *was* provided by her individual analysis, which helped her to regain a capacity for sustained enjoyment, whereupon she lost interest in encounter groups.

Analysis of other patients who have repeatedly participated in T-groups demonstrates how usual it is for them to be fascinated with the frustrating methods of T-group leaders. Such quasi-sadistic methods seem to activate and reinforce already present highly charged masochistic fantasies. Indeed, for most people, being wrenched back and forth among intensely cathected libidinal attachments in brief, repeated sessions of an encounter group seems to promise more damage than enrichment inasmuch as there is often a retreat to shallow unstable love relationships, as already noted.

XX Analytic Multiple Therapy

THE current demand for psychotherapy by patients for whom it has been recommended exceeds anything that the number of qualified psychotherapists now available can handle on a one-to-one basis. Group work, which enables one therapist to establish and maintain a supportive therapeutic arena for several patients simultaneously, offers at least a partial solution to this dilemma, and from this point of view multiple therapy, in which two or more therapists meet with a single patient, might seem to be an extravagant use of professional time.

However, when the group psychotherapy is analytic the demands on the energies of the therapist are somewhat heavier than they are in individual analysis. He must give both free-floating attention and considerable reflection to the task of following and usefully understanding the flow of events in the group-analytic process. To respond to it either nonverbally or by interpretations or other comments, and to give the necessary thought to it in intervals between group sessions has been, in my experience, more difficult and time-consuming than in the case of individual analysis; the need to master relevant aspects of the life experience of each of a number of patients also makes analytic work with a group more taxing.

Some therapists in group-analytic therapy, as in individual analysis, misuse the concept of the unconscious as the instrument of perception, and simply "float" in the group-analytic situation, unselectively communicating their insights. Otto Fenichel (1941) speaks of this deficiency as it appears in individual analysis:

Thus there is lacking the oscillation from intuition to understanding and knowledge which alone makes it possible to arrange in a larger context the material which has been understood with the help of the analyst's unconscious.

He also discusses the contrasting kind of error that can occur in individual analysis when intuition and empathy are bypassed and the patient is led to dwell altogether in a shadow world of words and concepts.

A constant important task of the analyst is to steer a course between the Scylla of talking instead of experiencing, and the Charybdis of unsystematic "free-floating" that corresponds to the "acting-out" of the patient and is not comprehended by a reasoning power that keeps ulterior aims in view.

It is this "free-floating" of the therapist, as well as his occasional acting-out with other participants, that characterizes today's frequently undisciplined group therapy; intellectual discussions, therapeutically sterile, are less usual. It seems as though the hard intellectual work involved in effective analytic group therapy has driven many group therapists into unreason, although, of course, they support their self-indulgent practices by much rationalization. Nevertheless, even with a well-balanced and disciplined psychotherapeutic approach—when the therapist balances intuition and empathy with his understanding and deals adequately with his own noxious counter-transference—the process may be stalemated by the development of a consolidated resistance in one of the patients.

When such a stalemate does occur in either individual or group psychotherapy with an analytic orientation, or a patient presents an impasse early in treatment, a shift to multiple therapy may prove more economical in the long run. Its therapeutically useful interactional possibilities were early and systematically exploited by Rudolf Dreikurs (1950), who claimed for its use in some situations the economy of more rapid improvement.

When multiple therapy is used within the Adlerian conceptual framework the therapists concern themselves with understanding the patient's life-style and goals, questioning him in an effort to understand his value system and the means he employs to move toward his objectives. Presently they discuss their findings while the patient listens, possibly intervening to provide additional information or to substitute his explanation for those the therapists offer jointly or individually. The three people in a room together soon unite in a common effort to understand the patient's motivation and methods, the possibly fictive nature of some of his goals, and the means whereby he may establish more effective ways of accomplishing his realistic designs.

Greenbank (1964) describes the use of multiple therapy within the framework of Freudian analytically-oriented psychotherapy. His patients were overtly psychotic or burdened by psychosomatic problems or severe character disorder. Greenbank notes that although this is not a universally applicable technique it is sometimes a successful tool for use when individual psychotherapy is difficult or intolerable for the patient. He adds that the technique requires a high order of psychotherapeutic competence, particularly in view of the complexity of the transference and counter-transference feelings that develop. Emotions are ventilated more freely and actively in a more rapidly developing transference than in individual therapy, which people who are comfortable only in a more intellectual atmosphere may find difficult to accept.

Greenbank describes the case of a 30-year-old white man, a scientific technician, who was referred for treatment because of stuttering and impotence. These symptoms appeared against the background of a schizoid personality with severe paranoid trends.

The patient was the younger of two children, having a sister four years his senior. His mother, a chronic invalid before her death, died when he was 14; after an absence of some years the father then cared for the boy, dying when his son became 23.

A Milquetoast after his stuttering began, the patient had earlier been given to overt expressions of rage now hidden below the surface. At the age of eight he threw a butcher knife at his sister and buried it four inches in her back. He bitterly denounced his mother on her deathbed, and while in his father's care gambled away much of his parent's hard-earned money.

He had often been separated from his parents, the complaining mother who had been warm and friendly before her stroke, and the father who imposed his will on his children.

He had seen many therapists, including psychoanalysts, psychiatrists, priests, counselors, and speech therapists, some of whom were women. He abruptly terminated any treatment psychologically sophisticated enough to threaten the uncovering of anything important, and on the other hand whenever treatment seemed unproductive he stopped after a few months on the grounds of his disappointment. He was reluctant to accept a suggestion to try psychoanalytic psychotherapy, but agreed in desperation. Shortly after beginning, he expressed a liking for his therapist and the intention of seeking a woman therapist to work with his impotence, denying the homosexual panic that motivated this flight from therapy as it had earlier retreats. He dreamed of being chased by male persons in authority and balked at returning to treatment, but agreed to continue when dual therapy to include a woman therapist was suggested.

The co-therapist chosen was a mature, motherly woman, not overtly seductive. She was well recommended by the trust imposed in her by the many acutely psychotic patients with whom she had worked extensively for many years. Still suspicious, the patient agreed to a single visit "to meet the lady doctor", and visibly relaxed in her presence. After a few cautious questions he was comfortable in a one-to-one relationship which actually excluded the male therapist, and made available much material in which he had a heavy investment of emotion—childhood memories, dream analysis, and considerable transference affect. His self-destructive social behavior improved after regression in this stage of treatment; further regression led him to "fire" the male therapist and to continue in a warm relationship with the female therapist, who reported to her colleague and worked under his supervision. The patient disclosed a repressed memory of his mother's desire that he be a girl in order to replace an older sister who had died before his birth; he had not previously remembered the existence of the dead child.

An abrupt change in their relationship occurred when the therapist happened to come to their session wearing a red skirt. Panic-stricken, the patient demanded a private interview with the male therapist, whom he had not mentioned for some time, and to whom he wanted to confide his indignation over "that whore" who, he now believed, had his seduction and humiliation as a goal. Abreaction continued for several weeks although he became conscious that this was projection—"What I want is to show my penis to prove I'm a male . . . at least I've got a penis to show." As he relaxed he felt closer to the male therapist, but again experienced homosexual panic, "inviting" the female co-therapist to return to the therapeutic situation. This transference relationship did not duplicate that present at the outset of treatment; this time the patient made a vigorous verbal attack on the male therapist while talking to his colleague. Transferring his rage from woman to man, he described the latter as being cold, demanding, without understanding, and chiefly interested in his fee. "Without a woman I couldn't talk; I'd be at his mercy."

Productive analytic work in the dual situation became possible after several months during which both therapists obviously withstood his attacks and offered no retaliation. He then spoke of his treatment with the man and woman as "a different home where the son is expected this time to be successful in growing into a man, and therefore can do so". During this time he became notably more successful in his profession.

After several years of treatment the serious illness of the female co-therapist, which required her extended absence, further demonstrated the value of the dual therapy. Experience of a loss like that he had suffered when his mother died was a great emotional blow to the patient, who turned to his remaining therapist with the declaration that he would rather kill himself than go to a stranger.

He worked through the mourning process and uncovered a repressed memory. "When I was four, my mother left me; she had gone on a train. The picture of my crying outside a house is vivid." He showed increased maturity as therapy continued. Although he had been terrified of women, he began to date, and although initially he had a neurotic relationship with an unsuitable woman he achieved orgasm with her, and ultimately made a good marriage with another woman. As he wound up his treatment he dreamed, "I'm a javelin thrower. I do well; Mother gives me a blue ribbon, and Dad is proud." The convulsive movements of the face and the stammering disappeared.

It had been possible to keep this paranoid patient in productive treatment only because a second member of the therapeutic team was available whenever sexual or hostile transference stirrings became intensified and generated overwhelming anxiety. Had his treatment been dyadic he would have fled.

As a matter of fact, dual therapists are often found in group therapy, including group-analytic psychotherapy in which training procedures often permit a neophyte to sit in as an observer and later to act as co-therapist, regularly discussing the events of each group session with its conductor-supervisor. Supervisors of both group and individual therapies often find themselves engaged in "dual therapy" in spite of the fact that they may never have seen the patient personally. Patients may become aware of changes in the therapeutic method and in the therapist himself as a result of supervision. As Franz Alexander (1950) pointed out, the supervisor's shadow often seems to peer over the therapist's shoulder. Indeed, many such shadows are likely to backstop the trainee psychotherapist as he works with the patient whose progress he reports. The teaching psychiatrist often takes on the shape of the grandfather in the transference–counter–transference projections of the therapeutic course he is supervising.*

In one case a young male patient in analytic therapy exhibited after a year of biweekly psychotherapy and a recent three-month period of particularly productive sessions a persistent unyielding resistance in argumentation with no progress.

This failed to yield to the continuing efforts of the supervisor and the male trainee therapist. Material proffered by the therapist made it clear that his patient entertained gross fears of "being screwed" and felt obliged to "be on top of" the therapist, who would somehow repeatedly fail to analyze defenses and to elucidate fantasies adequately. When he did approach the fantasies he failed to show their infiltration in and distortion of the patient's perception of his situation in therapy.

There seemed then to be little chance of reaching the patient's morbid apprehension in this situation. The supervisor met with the therapist and the patient together in the therapist's office. Although he had previously agreed enthusiastically to the meeting the patient shortly showed evidence of perceiving the visit as an unwelcome intrusion. Faced with the emergence in the flesh of the consultant who had been hitherto only imagined, he allied himself with his therapist in an attempt to ward off an imagined threat to both of them in the three-cornered session, which thus became very lively and productive.

* See also David L. Mayer's discussion of transference splits that may arise when more than one physician is involved in the treatment of a patient, and the possible replication of constellations of relationship in the patient's childhood experience. In "A blind spot in clinical research", *The Psychiatric Quarterly*, 1972, No. 3, pp. 384–401.

It became possible to discuss his attempted alliance with his older brother during his childhood to defend himself against the threats he imagined his father was making, and the failure of this attempt and his subsequent feeling that he was the butt of them both. The fantasies of "being screwed" and the anxiety connected with them were more adequately elucidated as he was able to understand that he saw the supervisor as an intruding castrating primal father image. The discrepancy between the actual situation in which the therapist was attempting to help him, and his fear of being sexually attacked by him was discussed with examples of his arguments and the words with which he chose to express himself. During the session the patient recalled the problem of his delayed speech in childhood (he later became very fluent) and remembered that when he did first speak, at the age of three, it was to threaten to stick a kitchen knife into his father's buttocks.

The therapist later noted that his transference position shifted from that of a threatening father to that of a domineering, directive, and unloving mother. The patient began to recall feelings about his young mother. The therapist noted that besides the decrease in excessive transference distortion, the shift in transference objects was the most striking result to be observed in the sessions that followed the one in which the consultant had been physically present with the patient and his therapist.

Thomas Hegarty (1972) reports the case of a housewife he treated as a resident at the University of Virginia whose short-term treatment for psychogenic bronchial asthma was relieved of a therapeutic impasse by permitting her to relate to his supervisor as co-therapist. Much of the therapy in this case was not conducted in joint sessions, but with the patient *vis-à-vis* one of the two therapists at a time. In this case the patient's perception of her two physicians as polar opposites greatly hastened the resolution of her problem.

The terms "good therapist" and "bad therapist" are used to convey the patient's emotional viewpoint and not a state of therapeutic grace. . . . In this case each therapist had a different conception of his role, therapist G planning to deal with the patient's "here and now" problems, with therapist B concentrating on the psychogenetic reconstruction of her symptom formation. G did indeed deal with many of her current problems, including her marriage, seeing her jointly with her husband; and B did gradually reconstruct pertinent psychodynamic issues.

Because of the differences in their personalities and techniques, however, the patient began almost at once to view the senior therapist as benevolent, comforting, nonthreatening, and the resident as aggressive, hurtful, and dangerous.

It was hypothesized that her asthma resulted from aggressive drive derivatives pathologically channeled into bronchiolar hypersecretion and constriction. Her ambivalence toward her parents, particularly toward her father, interfered with normal grief processes when they died; an underlying pathological response of mourning seemed evident in the appearance of asthma symptoms in the absence of normal grief manifestations. According to this formulation, relief of the asthma would require reactivation and working-through of the arrested grief process, with abreaction and rechanneling of aggressive drive derivates. Dual therapy with one "bad" and one "good" therapist provided an excellent mechanism for accomplishing this. The patient was able to direct her previously well-defended hostility toward the "bad" therapist while retaining the "good" therapist's support. In this way the transference was split, focused, and intensified as it could not have been with one therapist alone, since with only one therapist the surfacing of intensely hostile and destructive feelings within the context of brief psychotherapy means to the patient that if he shows these he will lose the therapist's support. If the therapist recognizes this and encourages the patient to "let go of whatever you are feeling" (presumably anger) he conveys this message, "I know you are angry but I am allowing you to be angry at me so that you will get better." This approach has the potential pitfall of defusing the patient's anger by making it permissible or contrived.

With separate good–bad therapists such dilemmas are avoided. The patient quickly learns which therapist wounds and which soothes; his hate–love toward them is real to him in a way that makes the transference that much more intense.

The need for both therapists to fit comfortably into their roles requires some congruency of personality with therapeutic approach. This patient initially saw her resident-therapist B as bad because he used a head-on attack on her defenses, with little consideration for her pain. Conversely, the supervisor G was seen as good because he was more gentle, less aggressive, and more willing to bide his time and lend support. Their personalities substantiated their role assignments, since B was physically and therapeutically "lean and hungry" while G was professionally well-established and had a physique and air of benevolence that had prompted his students to call him "coach".

Therapist B told the patient to begin, and met her repeated requests for more structure with silence. He ostentatiously yawned when she embarked on a long account of her asthma in its medical aspects, and told her that he would begin listening only when she stopped talking trivia. When she failed to come to B's office for her next appointment B went to get her, charged her with wasting time for both of them, and indicated that if she were not serious about therapy she could get out. However, when she later began to express genuine sadness over the death of her parents he told her, "O.K. You are working hard now. Go on." B's contract with her could be stated as—"It is your job to explore and work through the emotional issues involved with your asthma. It is my job to goad you to that task, to keep you at it and help you with it no matter how painful it seems at that time."

Following her first session with B the patient "confessed" to G all of her "past sins," mostly youthful sexual indiscretions that had preyed on her mind but that she had not felt able to disclose, not even to the psychiatrist who had treated her for nine months. It was obvious that it was stressful interaction with B that had helped precipitate her opening up to therapist G. When he responded to her "confession" with support and reassurance she experienced great relief. This pattern of stress (interaction with therapist B) and relief (interaction with therapist G) was repeated often throughout her brief course. Therapist G, however, provided the support necessary to keep her in therapy, and simultaneously promoted further movement by not taking sides in the conflict with therapist B, and continuing to help her with her current problems. The risk of driving the patient out of therapy with an approach like therapist B's is considerable unless countering forces of support are built into the treatment situation. As the patient put it, "If it weren't for Dr. G I would have left the hospital."

This is not to say, however, that resolution of transference did not occur; a tempering of transferences occurred concurrently with her turning the corner in her treatment (decreased asthma attacks, increased sadness and depression). Despite his continuing aggressiveness, therapist B seemed now to be helping her. At the end of her sessions with him she began to say, "I hate to come here but my asthma feels better when I leave." Conversely, therapist G lost some of his over-idealized luster in her eyes. She summarized, "Dr. G is a really nice guy, but I think Dr. B helped me more". This indicates an integration of the underlying love–hate forces that, previously in conflict, had produced her asthma.

As in individual long-term psychoanalytic psychotherapy, the transference is the indicator of stage and progress of treatment, with resolution marking the end point. The difference lies in the fact that in the use of two therapists with contrasting roles transference may develop rapidly and intensely instead of proceeding cautiously until enough trust is established to allow for hostile expression. Also, the transference is made clear and concrete by focusing upon two different therapists who in reality have different personalities, approaches, and styles. This situation contrasts with the confusion inherent, at least initially, in having opposite love–hate strivings toward one therapist. In short, good–bad dual therapy is useful where brief intense abreaction and reintegration of opposing affects is sufficient to produce the desired change. In this case chronic hostility was mobilized and rechanneled from visceral musculature (bronchioles) to skeletal musculature (mostly vocal), thus relieving the asthma symptom.

It may be noted that Chinese efforts at thought reform have used a variation of good–bad technique with the goal of going beyond the rechannelizing of hostility to the effecting of broad changes in prisoners' attitudes and belief systems (Lifton, 1956). At the breaking point after a period of harassment the prisoner meets a sudden "calculated kindness" on the part of his interrogators. According to Lifton, "This shift in tactics invariably has tremendous effects; it can be a crucial step in the extraction of the confession and in the overall reform."

It is essential in dual therapy that both therapists remain united despite their differences in roles. This is facilitated by their common goal of getting the patient well, but is complicated by the tendency for rivalry to develop between them (Spitz and Kopp, 1957). If the patient manages to split the therapists and causes them to get into competition, progress will stop until this is resolved. These potential pitfalls make frequent discussions between therapists mandatory. In this case the sessions were generally brief, and although mainly for discussion of the psychodynamic progress, etc., and to keep abreast of the treatment plan, they were used also to defuse the therapists' negative counter-transferences, often by humor, the use of which was directly proportional to the amount of the patient's hostility. As the patient moved into the working-through phase the sessions became more businesslike.

Whitaker et al. (1949) have said that counter-transference is the fundamental force in brief psychotherapy. Dreikurs et al. (1952) cite as the chief difficulty in multiple therapies the relation the therapists have to each other. In fact, Gans (1962) questions whether the currents of co-therapists' strife may not sweep away the constructive potential; this comment is directed to the situation in which simultaneous rather than alternating interviews occur, but the same principle may be applied to the latter case.

When two therapists are not completely comfortable with their differences their strife will be conveyed to the patient, who will in turn have proportionate difficulty in integrating such differences.

This patient's internist, who had recommended her psychiatric treatment, was, with his continued commitment, a key in her overall course. Several times in the opening weeks of therapy she pressed him to return her to the medical ward and make more diagnostic tests, but despite her exacerbated symptoms he stuck by the treatment plan. Dr. G maintained close liaison with him, explaining the treatment plan and its progress, and preventing a possible psychiatric–medical split. Residents and students making rounds with the internist were, however, sympathetic with the patient's doubts, but abandoned their skepticism when success seemed assured. At a joint conference for therapist, internist, and students, the students showed great interest in the psychotherapeutic methods that had been used. The ward staff served mainly as an extension of therapist G's support; a review of the case summary showed that the ward was an important arena for abreaction throughout the course of the treatment. When the patient verbalized anger against therapist B she was supported by ward personnel for her honesty, and encouraged to express anger directly to B. When she did this during the last minutes of her last session with him—"Thank you for all of your help, but I have really thought all along that you are a bastard"—she was congratulated on the ward for her "courage", particularly by her fellow patients.

XXI Coda—in Perspective

THERE is ample justification for seeing the rise of the encounter-group movement as another instance of the success of an idea whose time has come. The New Morality demands that the individual lose himself in the shared life. One should "hang loose", not "hang back". But to admit that the encounter group can provide a kind of short-lived symptomatic relief for the discomforts and disappointments of life today is not, however, to endorse it as a remedy for the disease itself, nor to hold that its benefits outweigh the damage that it can bring about.

Oswald Spengler (1926) pointed out eloquently and forcefully that all great cultures pass through a cycle of birth and decay. There are optimistic cultural historians who see the possibility of rebirth (Toynbee, 1934) for our Western world, and encourage us to think of contemporary turmoil as an evolutionary phase of progress rather than as the penultimate phase of decay and regression. It can be useful to weigh novel behavior patterns against the polarity of these possibilities.

The encounter group's attractiveness can be specifically related to current conditions in hidden as well as obvious ways. The movement is one evidence of protest against the regressive depersonalized pressures of a mechanized and materialistic world in which the individual feels severely undervalued and undernourished, and exploited and manipulated by faceless forces with the indifference and inexorability of a juggernaut. The concept of time as a leisurely unfolding has been violated by an advanced technology, and the concept of the natural world as an immutable and somehow consoling setting for human life can no longer be entertained. While there is nothing new about loneliness and cruelty and ennui, many cultures had provided elaborate myths as collective defenses against them; in contemporary life such collective defenses seem to have been either abandoned in scorn or thwarted by present circumstances of mechanized work and urban crowding in poorly designed, vast metropolitan complexes.

It is sadly paradoxical that in a now overpopulated and crowded milieu the individual tends to share his life with fewer and fewer other people, and to be less and less confident of his own identity in consequence. The encounter group promises, implicitly or explicitly, the chance to achieve a richer awareness of one's emotional possibilities, and an extension of empathic sensibility to the communications and responses of others; it offers a chance for the alienated and numb to experience companionship and feeling, to become reciprocally involved in the life around them. But when body contact and display are encouraged as a way to achieve instant closeness, the aim-inhibition of instinctual impulses may be threatened, or even undone by regression.

The type of regression seen in groups has been repeatedly discussed throughout these pages. We have often noted that limits on regression are set in group-analytic psychotherapy, and are firmly maintained by the discriminative activity of the conductor. Group therapy is generally monitored—intentionally or unintentionally—to prevent excessive regression. Yet it is clear that groups can evince the most startling and deep regressions either through the influence of strong leadership or the contagion of strong emotion—or both. Even when the group as a whole may not be obviously acting-out in regression some of its members may enlarge upon what is only a tendency of the group and exhibit personal behavior that must be judged psychotic.

Regression to childish, immature behavior on the part of the group as a whole constitutes the same gross impediment to therapy that it does to any other group task; it may occasion intense irrational anxiety, collective murderous rage, or severe depression. All groups under stress may in some degree become regressive in one of their phases; this regression, under certain conditions of leadership, can reach deep and extraordinary levels. The lynch mob seen in the not too distant past in this country offers a highly interesting paradigm. Slavson (1964) pointed out that the emotions of anger and the patterns of hostility and withdrawal manifested in regression in group therapy are not all merely ontogenetically conditioned, but that some regressions receive powerful phylogenetic reinforcement.

We have noted that in group-analytic psychotherapy ontogenetic regression is usually not as deep as that occurring periodically in psychoanalysis. On this account the very early complex pairing dependency problems of nursing and early childhood are not revisited in intense transference in ways that can be readily utilized therapeutically by interpretation. For this reason some consider that symptom neuroses anchored in pre-genital fixations as much as in the phallic-oedipal phase of development are not so amenable to therapy in groups, whereas character disorders are more amenable in group-analytic psychotherapy. Since these character disorders are in various ways and in different degrees also anchored in oral, anal, and sadistic-phallic points of fixation, with correlative disturbances in object-relatedness, the subject deserves closer scrutiny.

Clinical findings indicate that, in general, the symptom neuroses, i.e. hysterical neurosis of the conversion type, obsessive-compulsive neurosis, phobic neurosis—and combinations of these—respond more adequately in individual psychoanalysis, whereas the character disorders, even some of those that are quite severe, respond at a perceptibly speedier rate in group-analytic psychotherapy in a properly composed group. Although regression in the more obvious transferences is less deep and intense than that reached at times in individual psychoanalysis, the impact of the group and the social interface at which this impact occurs is more intense in the group therapy situation. It is possible that this powerful impact is related to a primitive transference embedded in the phylogenetic struggle for survival, and is stimulated by the social reality of the therapy group. This primitive transference may remain largely unanalyzable.

In recent years many analytically-oriented psychiatrists have combined once-a-week individual sessions with once- or twice-weekly group sessions, and some of them claim more effective therapeutic leverage with otherwise refractory cases of neurotic character disorder. Through such mixed treatment the patient, of course, gets more total time and attention from the therapist, and this benefit is in addition to that provided by the mobilization of the "totemistic" transference in the group we have described, and the induced maternal transference in individual sessions.

The combined procedure raises the question of a possible primitive primal father residue in the transference with the male therapist in individual sessions. In my experience, it has certainly greatly increased the difficulties of analysis, but there is no doubt that it has vastly enhanced the power of suggestion, as in hypnosis. This enhancement is conducive to symptom relief in patients with symptom neuroses refractory to individual treatment, too. In pursuing analysis we want, of course, to secure as much adult-level therapeutic cooperation as we can so that the parentifying and primitive magical transferences may be raised to awareness. From the point of view of analysis, patients in a combined procedure may be too engulfed in a highly charged primitive transference, yet in the heat of this transference the symptoms may melt.

It would be highly interesting to learn about the experience of woman therapists in combined treatment procedures. The concern here would be the appearance of a transference saturated with the image of the Magna Mater. Edith Weigert-Vowinkel (1938) has written with scholarly speculation about this archetypal image.

Group-analytic psychotherapy must be differentiated by its analytic method from all encounter groups of whatever kind. It is further set apart by its utilization of regression that is regulated in the service of a possible enrichment of the ego. It involves the patient in an extended acquaintance with a few others; interpersonal closeness is gradually established through the ongoing sharing of experiences in which character and responses are tested and reacted to, and interactions carefully examined.

The hopeful search for a veritable renaissance of spontaneous, compassionate, fully aware, and life-loving man deserves our sympathy, especially when we realize how despairingly so many have lost their bearings in the fog of today's world. But in spite of recognizing that it arises from desperation, one cannot endorse one-sided and almost thoughtless protest that loses itself in the mouthing of slogans and clichés, chanting and dancing, and acting in unbalanced excitement and sensationalism. The dissociation of feeling and sensation from cognition, the dissociation of frenetic week-end episodes from the social and political issues of our challenged and challenging common daily world, betray regression and hysteria. In the interpenetration of opposites the episodic encounter group can readily become an escape from a more courageous humanism—and often even an addictive escape.

Knowledge of the prehistory of early relationships of the reproductive family and the clan (gens) remains very shaky. In *Totem and taboo* Freud (1913) discussed some of the apparent resemblances between the mentality of surviving primitive tribes such as the Australian aborigines and that of neurotics within Western society, noting the universal horror of incest in relation to exogamy. The human family gradually came to exert its pressure to induce the emergence of aim-inhibitions and the possibility of stable relationships with fellow humans outside the family. The clan insisted upon and enabled symbolic transformations of primitive primal impulses which have evolved in our society into higher sublimations, including means whereby we communicate with others. The frank "mind-blowing" efforts of some encounter groups are extraordinarily revolutionary, seeking to overthrow the very basis of civilization, and exulting in an apotheosis of violence, an idolatry of sensuality, and a strident anti-intellectualism. All of this regressive mindlessness leads to "copping out" and fails to contribute toward any progressive amelioration of the anachronistic deficiencies of our society, contrary to the claims of some proponents of bizarre marathon groups—who also advocate abolition of the family.

The reduction of superstition and neurotic guilt, necessary if we are to become more humane, does not demand the death of the family but its support and education. The encounter group, with its open orientation to sensation and feeling, its stress on authentic individual identity, and its denigration of social rigidity and protocol, is nevertheless attractive to those who see all our recently discarded social imperatives as hypocritical. Having condemned the family pattern and all conventional formality as a perversion, they feel hopeful that spontaneity, genuine delight, and unfailing compassion and understanding will flow from free human exchange. But, having broken the vessel they found too unyielding, they now try to carry water in a sieve. Small wonder that the encounter group itself in time becomes stylized; role-playing and ritual reappear in new forms, and patent hypocrisy appears in the denial of responsible adult dimensions of experience. Participants may actually feel even *more* anxiety and distress through the breakthrough of ideational representations of primitive primal impulses in the presence of others outside the group, and be even less competent and happy than before in relationships with other people. Having been overly inhibited, some now feel so threatened by their newly released impulses that they withdraw to solitary safety—or they act out in so uncontrolled and uncontrollable a fashion as to repel those they would woo. In some isolated and notorious instances psychopathic leadership and the misuse of drugs have led groups to engage in the regressive behavior of a marauding clan. Thus, the excitement, intensified sensation, and heightened—but narrowed—awareness, the conditions that triggered the rebellion are replicated in caricature. The short-term, altogether transient character of encounter sessions, and the absence of adequate psychiatric guidance and benevolent leadership contribute to disappointing and circular outcomes. Like Christmas, a movement with a core of psychic promise has been commercialized.

Max Rosenbaum (1972) has recently written an overview of group psychotherapy which criticizes over-eager acceptance of the encounter movement. He concludes in words which we can profitably borrow for conclusion here:

> Psychotherapists who work with groups are on the "firing line". They cannot escape the provocative insights of patients. They will be attacked by the far right and the far left—particularly as they point out that the individual should explore his own capacities and still remain non-accepting of a culture which needs reconstruction.

Bibliography

Abercrombie, M. L. J. 1960. *The anatomy of judgment: an investigation into the processes of perception and reasoning*. London: Hutchinson & Co., Ltd.

— — 1971. Aims and techniques of group teaching. In *Society for Research into Higher Education Working Party on Teaching Methods*, publication 2, 2nd ed. With appendix by M. L. J. Abercrombie and P. M. Terry. London: SRHE, Ltd.

Abrahams, J. and Varon, E. 1953. *Maternal dependency and schizophrenia.* New York: International Universities Press.

Abse, D. W. with Estes, M. 1952. Hospital atmosphere improved and patient recoveries increased by group psychotherapy. *Mental Hospitals* 3 (9): 4.

— — with Jessner, L. 1962. The psychodynamic aspects of leadership. In *Excellence and leadership in a democracy*, ed. S. R. Graubard and G. Holton. New York: Columbia University Press.

— — 1966. *Hysteria and related mental disorders.* Baltimore: Williams & Wilkins. Bristol: John Wright & Sons.

— — 1971. *Speech and reason.* Charlottesville, Virginia: University Press of Virginia.

Ackerman, N. W. 1945. Some theoretical aspects of group psychotherapy. In *Group psychotherapy: a symposium*, ed. Jacob L. Moreno. New York: Beacon House.

— — 1966. Family therapy. In *American handbook of psychiatry*, ed. S. Arieti, Vol. III, Chapter 14. New York: Basic Books, Inc.

Adler, A. 1917. *Neurotic constitution.* Tr. B. Glueck and G. Lind. New York: Moffat Yard & Co.

— — 1927. *Understanding human nature.* New York: Greenberg.

Alexander, F. 1950. Teaching psychodynamics. *American Journal of Orthopsychiatry* 17 (4): 605.

Alger, I. 1971. Insight and involvement in individual therapy through videotape confrontation. In *Techniques of therapy*, ed. J. Masserman, pp. 20–36. (Vol. XVIII of *Science and psychoanalysis*.) New York and London: Grune & Stratton.

Ammon, G. 1971. Zur Situation der psychoanalytischen Ausbildung. *Dynamische Psychiatrie* ("Dynamic Psychiatry"), 4. Jarhgang: 2. Quartal. Berlin: Pinel Publikationem.

Anthony, E. J. 1968. Critique of "Accelerated interaction: a time-limited approach based on the brief, intensive group" by F. H. Stoller. *International Journal of Group Psychotherapy* 18: 220–235.

Aristotle. On memory and reminiscence ("De memoria et reminiscentia"). Tr. G. I. Beane. In *The works of Aristotle*, Vol. I. Vol. 8 of *The Great Books of the Western World*, ed. Robert Maynard Hutchins. Chicago: Encyclopedia Britannica Inc. (1952).

Armstrong, S. W. and Rouslin, S. 1963. *Group psychotherapy in nursing practice*. New York: The Macmillan Company.

Back, K. W. 1972. *Beyond words: the story of sensitivity training and the encounter movement*. Russell Sage Foundation. New York: Basic Books, Inc.

Badtke, S. A. 1972. We believe you do not have to be sick to get better. *Wisconsin Mental Health Journal*.

Bakshy, A. 1945. The theatre of Maxim Gorki. In *Seven plays of Maxim Gorki*. Tr. A. Bakshy and P. S. Nathan. New Haven: Yale University Press.

Baruch, A. 1969. Art therapy as related to group therapy. In *Group therapy today*, ed. H. M. Ruitenbeek. New York: Atherton Press.

Bateson, G.; Jackson, D.; Haley, J.; and Weakland, J. 1956. Toward a theory of schizophrenia. *Behavioral Science* 1: 251–264.

Battegay, R. 1971. Group dynamics. In *Psychodynamic approach to group therapy and to psychotherapy of psychotics*. Acta Psychiatrica Scandinavica, Supplementum 224. Copenhagen: Munksgaard.

Beckett, S. 1954. *Waiting for Godot*. New York: Grove Press.

Benedek, T. 1959. Parenthood as a developmental phase: a contribution to the libido theory. *Journal of the American Psychoanalytic Association* 7 (3): 389–417.

Berger, M. M. 1971. Self-confrontation through video. *American Journal of Psychoanalysis* 31 (1): 48–58.

Berger, M. M. 1972. *The use of videotape in group analytic theory.* Presented at the 2nd European Symposium on Group Analysis, May 12, 1972, in London.

Bettelheim, B. 1950. *Love is not enough: the treatment of emotionally disturbed children.* New York: The Free Press of Glencoe.

—— 1960. *The informed heart: autonomy in a mass age.* New York: The Free Press of Glencoe.

Bibring, G. L.; Dwyer, T. F.; Huntington, D. S.; and Valenstein, A. F. 1961. A study of the psychological processes in pregnancy and of the earliest mother–child relationship. Appendix B: Glossary of defenses. *The Psychoanalytic Study of the Child* 16: 62–72.

Bierer, J. and Haldane, F. P. 1941. A self-governed patients' social club in a public mental hospital. *Journal of Mental Science* 87 (July).

Bion, W. R. 1961. *Experiences in groups.* New York: Basic Books, Inc.

Blos, P. 1962. *On adolescence: a psychoanalytic interpretation.* New York: The Free Press.

Bonnard, A. 1960. The primal significance of the tongue. *International Journal of Psychoanalysis* 41: 301–307.

Bowen, M.; Dysnia, R.; and Basamania, B. 1959. The role of the father in families with a schizophrenic patient. *American Journal of Psychiatry* 115: 1017–1020.

Breuer, J. *See* Flugel, J. C., *A hundred years of psychology: 1833–1933.*

Burrow, T. 1926. The group method of analysis (German). *Imago* 12: 211–222.

—— 1927. The group method of analysis. *Psychoanalytic Review* 14: 268–280.

—— 1927. *The social basis of consciousness: a study in organic psychology.* In The International Library of Psychology, Philosophy, and Scientific Method. London: Kegan Paul, Trench, Trubner & Co., Ltd. New York: Harcourt Brace.

—— 1928. The basis of group-analysis or the analysis of the reactions of normal and neurotic individuals. *The British Journal of Medical Psychology* 8: 198–206.

—— 1950. *The neurosis of man: an introduction to a science of human behavior.* London: Routledge & Kegan Paul.

—— 1953. *Science and man's behavior: the contribution of phylobiology.* New York: Philosophical Library.

Burrow, T. 1958. *A search for man's sanity—the selected letters of Trigant Burrow*. Ed. by Committee of Lifwynn Foundation, E. Galt, chairman. Foreword by Sir Herbert Read. New York: Oxford University Press.

Chappell, M. N.; Stefano, G. G.; Rogerson, G. S.; and Pike, F. H. 1936. The value of group psychological procedures in the treatment of peptic ulcer. *American Journal of Digestive Disease and Nutrition*, Vol. 3.

Chmiel, A. 1972. *Psychotherapy in mental retardation: a review*. Residency thesis at the University of Virginia.

Corsini, R. G. 1955. Historic background of group psychotherapy: a critique. *Group Psychotherapy* 8 (3): 219–226.

Cotzin, M. 1948. Group psychotherapy with mentally defective problem boys. *American Journal of Mental Deficiency* 53: 268–283.

Dreikurs, R. 1950. Techniques and dynamics of multiple psychotherapy. *Psychiatric Quarterly* 24: 788–799.

— — 1951. The unique social climate experienced in group psychotherapy. *Group Psychotherapy* 8 (3): 292–299.

— — with Shulman, B. H. and Mesak, H. 1952. Patient–therapist relationship in multiple psychotherapy: I. Its advantages for the therapist. *Psychiatric Quarterly* 26: 219–227.

Durkheim, E. 1897. *Le suicide: étude de sociologie*. Paris: Felix Alcan.

Edelson, M. 1964. *Ego psychology, group dynamics and the therapeutic community*. New York: Grune & Stratton.

— — 1967. The socio-therapeutic function in a psychiatric hospital. *Journal of the Fort Logan Mental Health Center* 4: 1–45.

Eisenberg, L. 1963. Preventive psychiatry: if not now, when? *World Mental Health*, Vol. 15.

Ellis, H. 1936. *Love and pain*, Vol. I, Part II. New York: Random House.

Ellul, J. 1965. *Propaganda: the formation of men's attitudes*. Tr. K. Kellen and J. Lerner. New York: Alfred A. Knopf.

Erikson, E. 1956. The problem of ego identity. *Journal of the American Psychoanalytic Association* 4: 56–121.

— — 1959. Identity and the life cycle. *Psychological Issues* I (1): 129–133.

Esquirol, J. E. 1835. *Mental maladies, a treatise on insanity*. Tr. E. K. Hunt. Philadelphia: Lea & Blanchard, 1845.

Ewing, J. A.; Long, V.; and Wenzel, G. G. 1961. Concurrent group psychotherapy of alcoholic patients and their wives. *International Journal of Group Psychotherapy* 11 (3): 329–338.

Ezriel, H. A. 1950. A psychoanalytic approach to group treatment. *British Journal of Medical Psychology* 23: 59–74.

Fenichel, O. 1941. *Problems of psychoanalytic technique*. Tr. D. Brunswick. Albany, New York: The Psychoanalytic Quarterly, Inc.

—— 1945. *The psychoanalytic theory of neurosis*. New York: W. W. Norton & Co. Inc.

Ferenczi, S. 1909. Introjection and transference. In *Sex in psychoanalysis: contributions to psychoanalysis*. Boston: Richard C. Badger (1922).

Fisher, L. D. and Wolfson, T. N. 1953. Group therapy of mental defectives. *American Journal of Mental Deficiency* 57: 463–476.

Flugel, J. C. 1921. *The psycho-analytic study of the family*. London: The Hogarth Press.

—— 1933. (re Breuer) *A hundred years of psychology: 1833–1933*, p. 194. London: Duckworth.

Fortin, J. N. and Abse, D. W. 1956. Group psychotherapy with peptic ulcer. *International Journal of Group Psychotherapy* 6 (4): 383–391.

Foulkes, S. H. 1948. *Introduction to group-analytic psychotherapy*. London: William Heinemann Medical Books.

—— 1960. The application of group concepts to the treatment of the individual in the group. In *Topical problems of psychotherapy*, Vol. II, Chapter 12. Basle and New York: Karger.

—— 1964. *Therapeutic group analysis*. New York: International Universities Press, Inc.

Frank, J. D. 1954. Group psychotherapy with outpatients. *Tri-state Medical Journal* 1 (12).

—— 1961. The role of influence in psychotherapy. In *Contemporary psychotherapies*, ed. M. I. Stein. New York: The Free Press.

Freud, S. 1911. Psychoanalytic notes upon an autobiographical account of a case of paranoia. In *Collected papers*, Vol. III, ed. E. Jones. London: Hogarth Press (1943).

—— 1913–14. Totem and taboo. In *The standard edition of the complete psychological works of Sigmund Freud*, Vol. XIII, ed. J. Strachey. London: Hogarth Press (1955).

—— 1921. Group psychology and the analysis of the ego. In *The standard edition of the complete psychological works of Sigmund Freud*, Vol. XVIII, ed. J. Strachey. London: Hogarth Press (1955).

Freud, S. 1938–1940. An outline of psychoanalysis. In *The standard edition of the complete psychological works of Sigmund Freud*, Vol. XXIII, ed. J. Strachey. London: Hogarth Press (1964).

Friedman, A. S. 1970. Family therapy as conducted in the home. In *Family process*, ed. N. W. Ackerman, pp. 102–110. New York: Basic Books, Inc.

Galton, F. 1874. *English men of science, their nature and nurture.* London: Macmillan & Co., Ltd.

Gans, R. 1962. Group co-therapists in the therapeutic situation. *International Journal of Group Psychotherapy* 12: 82.

Glassman, L. A. 1943. Is dull normal intelligence a contraindication for psychotherapy? *Smith College Studies in Social Work* 13: 275–298.

Goldhamer, H. and Marshall, A. W. 1953. *Psychosis and civilization: two studies in the frequency of mental disease.* Glencoe, Illinois: The Free Press.

Goldstein, K. 1939. *The organism: a holistic approach to biology derived from pathological data in man.* New York: American Book Co.

Gombrich, E. H. 1969. *Art and illusion: a study in the psychology of pictorial representation.* Princeton, N.Y.: Princeton University Press.

Gorky, M. *See* Bakshy, A.

Gottlieb, A. and Pattison, E. M. 1966. Married couples' group therapy. *Archives of General Psychiatry* 14 (2).

Gottschalk, L. A. 1966. Psychoanalytic notes on T-groups at human relations laboratory. *Comprehensive Psychiatry* 7: 472–487.

Greenbank, R. K. 1964. Psychotherapy using two therapists. *American Journal of Psychotherapy* 18 (3): 488–499.

Guttmacher, J. A. and Birk, L. 1971. Group therapy: What specific therapeutic advantages? *Comprehensive Psychiatry* 12 (6): 546–556.

Hadden, S. B. 1942. Treatment of the neuroses by class technic. *Annals of Internal Medicine* 16: 33–37.

—— 1944. Group psychotherapy: a superior method of treating larger numbers of neurotic patients. *American Journal of Psychiatry* 101: 68–73.

—— 1947. The utilization of a therapy group in teaching psychotherapy. *American Journal of Psychiatry* 103: 644–648.

Haley, J., ed. 1971. *Changing families: a family therapy reader.* New York: Grune & Stratton.

Hawkins, D. R.; Monroe, J. T., Jr.; Clarke, M. G.; and Vernon, C. R. 1966. Group psychotherapy as a method for the study of affects. In *The international handbook of group psychotherapy*, ed J. L. Moreno, A. Friedemann, R. Battegay, and Z. T. Moreno. New York: Philosophical Library, Inc.

Heffner, H. C. 1957. Pirandello and the nature of man. *The Tulane Drama Review I*(June): 23–40.

Hegarty, T. 1972. *"Good" therapist—"bad" therapist: treatment of psychogenic bronchial asthma.* Residency thesis at the University of Virginia.

Henderson, D. K. 1939. *Psychopathic states.* New York: W. W. Norton & Co., Inc.

Hertzler, J. O. 1965. *A sociology of language.* New York: Random House, Inc.

Hollingshead, A. B. and Redlich, F. C. 1958. *Community study.* New York: John Wiley & Sons, Inc.

Irmscher, W. F. and Hagemann, E. R. 1963. *The language of ideas.* Indianapolis: The Bobbs-Merrill Co., Inc.

Jackson, D. *See* Bateson, G.

Jaffe, S. L. and Scherl, D. J. 1969. Acute psychosis precipitated by T-group experience. *Archives of General Psychiatry* 21: 443–448.

James, W. 1890. *Principles of psychology.* New York: Henry Holt & Co., Inc. (New York: Dover Publications, 1950).

Jones, M. 1953. *The therapeutic community.* New York: Basic Books, Inc. (Published in England as *Social psychiatry*, 1952. London: Tavistock Publications.)

—— 1966. Therapeutic community practice. *American Journal of Psychiatry* 122: 1275–1279.

Jung, C. G. 1959. *Flying saucers: a modern myth of things seen in the skies.* London: Routledge & Kegan Paul, Ltd.

Kernan, A. B. 1958. Truth and dramatic mode in the modern theatre. *Modern Drama* 1 (2).

Khan, M. M. R. 1972. Apprenticeship, instruction and communication in psychoanalytic pedagogy. *Dynamische Psychiatrie* ("Dynamic Psychiatry") 5. Jahrgang: 1/2. Quartal: 1–21. Berlin: Pinel Publikationem.

Klapman, J. W. 1959. *Group psychotherapy, theory and practice*, 2nd ed. New York: Grune & Stratton.

Köhler, W. 1925. *The mentality of apes.* London: Kegan Paul, Trench, Trubner & Co., Ltd. New York: Harcourt Brace & Co. (1927).

—— 1929. *Gestalt psychology: an introduction to new concepts in modern psychology.* New York: Liveright Publishing Co.

Kreeger, L. 1972. *The background and application of large groups: a contribution to the open forum on the second day of the second European symposium on group analysis.* Presented at the Institute of Psychiatry: Group Analytic Society of London, in May 1972.

Krutch, J. W. 1953. *"Modernism" in modern drama.* Ithaca: Cornell University Press.

Kubie, L. S. 1971. A doctorate in psychotherapy. In *New horizons for psychotherapy,* ed. R. R. Holt. New York: International Universities Press, Inc.

Kuehn, J. L. and Crinella, F. 1969. Sensitivity training: interpersonal "overkill" and other problems. *American Journal of Psychiatry* 126 (6): 840–845.

LaBarre, W. 1964. Paralinguistics, kinesics and cultural anthropology. In *Approaches to semiotics,* ed. Thomas A. Sebiok et al. The Hague: Mouton & Co.

—— 1972. *The ghost dance: the origins of religion.* New York: Delta.

Lazell, E. W. 1921. The group treatment of dementia praecox. *Psychoanalytic Review* 8: 168–179.

Lawrence, D. H. 1927. Review of Burrow's "The social basis of consciousness". *The Bookman* 66: 314–317. (Republished in 1936 in *Phoenix: the posthumous papers of D. H. Lawrence.* New York: The Viking Press.)

Lewin, K. 1936. *Principles of topological psychology.* New York: McGraw-Hill, Inc.

—— 1939. Experiments in social space. *Harvard Educational Review* 9: 21–32.

—— 1951. *Field theory in social science.* New York: Harper & Row.

Liberman, R. P. 1971. Behavioural group therapy: a controlled clinical study. *British Journal of Psychiatry* 119: 535–544.

Lidz, T. 1963. *The family and human adaptation.* New York: International Universities Press.

—— 1967. Psychoanalytic theories of development and maldevelopment: some reconceptualizations. *American Journal of Psychoanalysis* 27: 115–126.

Lifton, R. J. 1956. "Thought reform" of Western civilians in Chinese Communist prisons. *Psychiatry* 19: 173–195.

Lin, T-Y. 1960. Social change and mental health. *World Mental Health* 12.

Luchins, A. S. 1964. *Group therapy, a guide.* New York: Random House.

MacClintock, L. 1951. *The age of Pirandello.* Bloomington: Indiana University Press.

McDougall, W. 1923. *An outline of psychology.* London: Methuen & Co., Ltd.

Mackay, D. 1932. *Extraordinary popular delusions and the madness of crowds.* New York: L. C. Page & Co.

Maine, T. F. 1946. The hospital as a therapeutic institution. *Bulletin of the Menninger Clinic* 10 (3).

Malzberg, B. 1959. Important statistical data about mental illness. In *American handbook of psychiatry*, ed. S. Arieti. New York: Basic Books, Inc.

Mann, P. H.; Beaber, J. D.; and Jacobson, M. D. 1969. The effect of group counseling on educable mentally retarded boy's self concept. *Exceptional Children* 35: 359–366.

Marsh, L. C. 1935. Group therapy and the psychiatric clinic. *Journal of Nervous and Mental Disease* 82: 381–393.

Mattsson, A. and Agle, D. P. 1973. Group therapy with parents of hemophiliacs: therapeutic process and observations of parental adaptation to chronic illness in children. *Journal of the American Academy of Child Psychiatry* 11: 558–571.

Mayer, D. L. 1972. A blind spot in clinical research. *Psychiatric Quarterly* No. 3: 384–401.

Meiers, J. G. 1945. Origins and development of group psychotherapy. In *Group psychotherapy: a symposium*, ed. J. L. Moreno. New York: Beacon House.

Menninger, K. with Mayman M. and Pruyser P. 1963. *The vital balance.* New York: The Viking Press, Inc.

Mill, J. 1829. *Analysis of the phenomena of the human mind.* London: Baldwin & Cradock.

Moreno, J. L. 1923. *Das Stegreiftheater.* Potsdam: Gustav Kiepenheuer Verlag. (In English *The theatre of spontaneity.* New York: Beacon House. 1947.)

— — ed. (with others). 1966. *The international handbook of group psychotherapy.* New York: Philosophical Library, Inc.

Nash, E. M.; Jessner, L.; and Abse, D. W. 1964. *Marriage counseling in medical practice.* Chapel Hill: The University of North Carolina Press.

National Committee on Prisons and Prison Labor. 1932. *Application of the group method to classification: introduction to group psychotherapy.* Washington, D.C.

Nunberg, H. and Federn, E., ed. 1962. *Minutes of the Vienna Psychoanalytic Society.* Introduction by H. Nunberg. New York: International Univsities Press, Inc.

Parloff, M. B. 1967. Advance in analytic group therapy. In *Frontiers of psychoanalysis,* ed. J. Marmor. New York: Basic Books, Inc.

Parloff, M. B.; Goldstein, N.; and Iflund, B. 1960. Communication of values and therapeutic change. *Archives of General Psychiatry* 2: 300–304.

Pavenstedt, E. (ed.) with Malone, C. A. 1967. *The drifters: children of disorganized lower-class families.* Boston: Little, Brown & Co.

Perls, F. 1969. *Gestalt therapy verbatim.* Lafayette, Calif.: Real People Press.

Piaget, J. 1929. *The child's conception of the world.* London: Kegan Paul, Trench, Trubner & Co., Ltd.

—— 1932. *The moral judgment of the child.* London: Kegan Paul, Trench, Trubner & Co., Ltd.

Pirandello, L. 1908. *L'umorismo,* 2nd (enlarged) ed. in Italian. Firenze: L. Battistelli.

—— 1922. *Naked masks: five plays.* New York: E. P. Dutton & Co., Inc. (1950–2).

Powdermaker, F. B., Frank, J. et al. 1953. *Group psychotherapy: studies in methodology of research and therapy.* Cambridge, Mass.: Harvard University Press.

Pratt, J. H. 1907. The class method of treating consumption in the homes of the poor. *Journal of the American Medical Association* 49: 755–759.

—— 1945. The group method in the treatment of psychosomatic disorder. In *Group psychotherapy: a symposium,* ed. J. L. Moreno. New York: Beacon House.

—— *See* also Luchins, A. S. 1964. *Group therapy, a guide.* New York: Random House.

Pumpian-Mindlin, E. 1969. Vicissitudes of infantile omnipotence. *Psychoanalytic study of the child* 24: 213–226.

Reich, I. O. 1969. *Wilhelm Reich: a personal biography.* Introduction by Paul Goodman. New York: St. Martin's Press.

Reich, W. 1933. *Massenpsychologie des Faschismus*, 2. Auflage. Copenhagen: Sexpol Verlag. (*The mass psychology of fascism*. Revised ed. Tr. T. P. Wolfe. New York: Orgone Institute Press, 1946.)

Rennie, T. A. C., Srole, L.; Opler, M. K.; and Langner, T. 1957. Urban life and mental health. *American Journal of Psychiatry* 113: 831.

Rioch, M. J. 1970. The work of Wilfred Bion on groups. *Psychiatry* 33 (1): 56–66.

Roger-Collard. *See* Ellis, H. 1936. *Love and pain*, Vol. I, Part II. New York: Random House.

Rogers, C. 1942. *Counseling and psychotherapy*. New York: Houghton Mifflin Co.

Rohéim, G. 1920. *Animism, magic, and the divine king*. New York: International Universities Press, Inc. (1972).

Rosenbaum, M. 1972. An overview of group psychotherapy and the present trend. *Group Process* 4 (2): 19–32.

Royal College of Physicians, 1944. Report of the Committee on Medical Education. London.

Sager, C. J. and Kaplan, H. S., eds. 1972. *Progress in group and family therapy*. New York: Bunner/Mazel.

Santayana, G. 1923. *Scepticism and animal faith*. New York: Charles Scribner's Sons.

Satir, V. M. 1966. Family therapy: an approach to the treatment of mental and emotional disorder. In *The international handbook of group psychotherapy*, ed. J. L. Moreno (with others). New York: Philosophical Library, Inc.

Schiff, S. B. and Glassman, S. M. 1969. Large and small group therapy in a state mental health center. *International Journal of Group Psychotherapy* 19 (2): 150–157.

Schilder, P. 1936. The analysis of ideologies as a psychotherapeutic method, especially in group treatment. *American Journal of Psychiatry* 93, 601–617.

Slavson, S. R. 1940. Group therapy. *Mental Hygiene* 24: 36–49.

— — 1964. *A text book in analytic group psychotherapy*. New York: International Universities Press, Inc.

Speers, R. and Lansing, C. 1964. *Group psychotherapy and psychotic children*. Chapel Hill: University of North Carolina Press.

Spengler, O. 1926–8. *Decline of the West*. Tr. with notes C. F. Atkinson, 2 vols. New York: Alfred A. Knopf, Inc.

Spitz, H. and Kopp, S. 1957. Multiple psychotherapy. *Psychiatric Quarterly Supplement* 31: 295–331.

Spotnitz, H. 1952a. Group therapy as a specialized psychotherapeutic technique. In *Specialized techniques in psychotherapy*, ed. G. Bychowski and G. L. Despert. New York: Basic Books, Inc.

—— 1952b. A psychoanalytic view of resistance in groups. *International Journal of Group Psychotherapy* 2: 3–9.

Stoller, F. H. *See* Anthony, E. J.

Stone, L. 1961. *The psychoanalytic situation*. New York: International Universities Press, Inc.

Strupp, H. H. 1960. *Psychotherapists in action: explorations of the therapist's contribution to the treatment process*. New York: Grune & Stratton.

Taintor, Z. 1970. Birth order and psychiatric problems in boot camp. *American Journal of Psychiatry* 126: 1604–1610.

Thomas, G. W. 1943. Group psychotherapy: a review of recent literature. *Psychosomatic Medicine* 5: 166–181.

Tilgher, A. 1928. *Studi sul teatro contemporaneo*. Rome: Libreria chi scienze e lettere.

Toffler, A. 1970. *Future shock*. New York: Random House.

Toynbee, A. 1934–54. *A study of history*. 10 vols. London: Oxford University Press.

Vittorini, D. 1935. *The drama of Luigi Pirandello*. Philadelphia: University of Pennsylvania Press.

Volkan, V. D. 1968. The introjection of and identification with the therapist as an ego-building aspect in the treatment of schizophrenia. *British Journal of Medical Psychology* 41: 369–380.

—— 1970. An experiment in the initial phase of education for the psychiatrist. *Nöro-psikiyatri Arsivi* 7: 25–33.

Volkan, V. D. and Hawkins, D. R. 1971a. The "fieldwork" method of teaching and learning clinical psychiatry. *Comprehensive Psychiatry* 12: 103–115.

—— 1971b. A field-work case in the teaching of clinical psychiatry. *Psychiatry in Medicine* 2: 160–176.

—— 1972. The learning group. *American Journal of Psychiatry* 128: 1121–1126.

Weakland, J. H. 1962. Family therapy as a research arena. *Family Process* 1: 63–68.

Weber, M. 1947. *The theory of social and economic organization*, Chapter III. Tr. A. M. Henderson and T. Parsons. New York: Oxford University Press.

—— 1954. Law in economy and society. In *Twentieth century legal philosophy series*, Vol. VI, ed. M. Rheinstein. Cambridge, Mass.: Harvard University Press.

Weigert-Vowinkel, E. 1938. The cult and mythology of the Magna Mater from the standpoint of psychoanalysis. *Psychiatry* 1: 347–378.

Weiss, P. 1966. *The persecution and assassination of Jean-Paul Marat as performed by the inmates of the asylum of Charenton under the direction of the Marquis de Sade*. Tr. Geoffrey Skelton. New York: Atheneum Publishers.

Wender, L. 1936. The dynamics of group psychotherapy and its application. *Journal of Nervous and Mental Disease* 84: 54–60.

Wertheimer, M. 1912. Experimentelle Studien über das Sehen von Bewegungen. *Zeitschrift für Psychologie* 61: 161–265.

—— 1925. *Drei Abhandlungen zur Gestaltheorie*. Erlangen: Philosophische Akademie, pp. iv–184.

Whitaker, C. A.; Warkenten, J.; and Johnson, N. L. 1949. A philosophical basis for brief psychotherapy. *Psychiatric Quarterly* 23: 439–443.

Wolf, A. 1963. The psychoanalysis of groups. In *Group psychotherapy and group function*, ed. M. Rosenbaum and M. Berger. New York: Basic Books, Inc.

—— et al. 1954. Sexual acting out in the psychoanalysis of groups. *International Journal of Group Psychotherapy* 4: 369–380.

Wolf, A.; Schwartz, E.; McCarty, E.; Goldberg, I. 1970. *Beyond the couch: dialogues in teaching and learning psychoanalysis in groups*. New York: Science House.

Wynne, L. C.; Ryckoff, I. M.; Day, J.; and Hirsch, S. S. 1958. Pseudomutality in the family relations of schizophrenics. *Psychiatry* 21: 205–220.

Yalom, I. D. 1966. A study of group therapy dropouts. *Archives of General Psychiatry* 14: 393–414.

—— with Lieberman, M. A. 1971. A study of encounter group casualties. *Archives of General Psychiatry* 25 (1): 16–30.

Ziferstein, I. and Grotjahn, M. 1957. Group dynamics of acting-out in analytic group psychotherapy. *International Journal of Group Psychotherapy* 7 (1): 77–85.

Zuk, G. H. 1972. *Family therapy: a triadic-based approach.* New York: Behavioral Publications, Inc.

Zweig, S. 1933. *Mental healers: Franz Anton Mesmer, Mary Baker Eddy, Sigmund Freud.* Tr. Eden and Cedar Paul. London: Cassell & Co., Ltd.

Subject Index

Index of Proper Names